VIETNAMESE

VIETNAMESE

SIMPLE VIETNAMESE FOOD
TO COOK AT HOME

Uyen Luu

Hardie Grant

BOOKS

INTRODUCTION

The Vietnamese way of asking, 'How are you?' is to say, 'Have you eaten rice yet?' Good fresh food is central to the lives of Vietnamese people, who tend to eat for the love of eating. Life is nothing without the enjoyment of good food.

Traditionally, grandmothers, aunts, uncles, fathers and mothers (including my own Má Nga, pictured here with my daughter Olive, aged 4) serve food as a way to show the strength of their love. As such, making a delicious meal brings Vietnamese people so much joy as it is a symbol of their feelings.

The heart of Vietnamese cooking is making do with what you have, and adapting to what is available and in season. This is exemplified in some familiar favourites of Vietnamese cuisine, such as *phở* and *bánh mì* – both of which are dishes taken and adapted from foreign occupiers. Some cooks go to great lengths to re-create the flavours of traditional dishes, but don't let that deter you because we can adapt and make the recipes our own.

The kitchen – be it large or small, dark or bright – is the backbone of the Vietnamese home; it is a place to find little triumphs and great liberation in cooking – to show the love. The dining table is a place of daily gatherings, to share delicious meals together with family, friends and neighbours; be it joyful or woeful, we must eat.

Eating alone is not frowned upon but will be greeted with sympathy. Food is for sharing. Every day, people eat together, enjoying either a modest or elaborate array of dishes. Eating is for pleasure, and gifting sweet and savoury snacks is a sign of friendship and kindness. On special occasions, like *Tết* (the Lunar New Year), eating certain foods is entwined with traditions and superstitions.

When you start to cook from this book, you will see that you only need a handful of essential ingredients for Vietnamese cooking and then you simply follow the rule of balancing sweet, sour, salty, umami, bitter and hot. Get the balance of these flavours right in all the recipes and you'll satisfy the palate and content hungry bellies. The dishes not only show off the flavours of fresh herbs and vegetables but display a rainbow of colours, tastes and textures. Vietnamese cuisine is happy and joyful – just like the Vietnamese themselves.

Many recipes in this book are designed for everyday meals. They use simple cooking techniques, such as pan-frying, blanching or one-pot cooking, and focus on letting the main ingredients – flavours of vegetables, herbs and spices – speak for themselves, with a simple sauce, perhaps, to bring them to life. You will find a combination of everyday meals from quick-to-make broths to family style sharing plates and one-pot wonders that are easy to prepare, adapt and enjoy.

My emphasis is on buying locally from responsible producers whenever possible and using ingredients that are easy to source for the young and old to enjoy every day of the week. There are sections reserved for weekends and feasts when you have a little more time to spend making dumplings, summer rolls and more elaborate brunches. This is known as eating for fun (*ăn chơi*). These recipes need a little more dedication and commitment but will be totally worth your time.

I have written the recipes with ease in mind: ease to get hold of the ingredients and to cook. I am happy for you to adapt the recipes and use what you can get hold of or replace what you can't. The idea is for you to have a skeleton of ingredients and methods to work with. If you can get hold of traditional Vietnamese herbs and ingredients, that's great. If not, don't let that stop you. The Vietnamese are famous for adapting their dishes to what is locally available and making use of every part of the ingredient, maximising on flavour and goodness while minimising waste. Waste is unheard of. Adapt, use everything up and make do.

This book is for you to eat well, eat fresh, eat responsibly and eat together, which promotes happiness and a feeling of well-being. Where appropriate, the recipes will contain ideas on substitutions so that you can make adjustments. I hope that this book gives you a great opportunity to learn how easy it is to achieve an authentic Vietnamese flavour. Even in those recipes that have several elements, the individual techniques are simple. For those longer recipes, the cooking time should be considered me-time and the finished dish a way of showing those closest to you that you adore them. Even at uncertain and worrying times, we can eat deliciously.

Happy cooking.

THE VIETNAMESE PANTRY

I am the classic hoarder of condiments and cupboard ingredients in case we go hungry. It is ingrained in me as a Vietnamese to always plan what my next meal is. I will always have a 10-kg (22-lb) bag of rice on standby.

I like to restock as soon as any essential storecupboard ingredient is half empty. At the very least, I always have something sweet (sugar, honey), something sour (vinegar), something hot (chilli sauce), something salty (soy sauce) and something umami (fish sauce) – a bottle of fish sauce is the staple of Vietnamese cooking – in my pantry.

Then I like to have a fresh supply of ginger root, shallots, garlic, lemongrass and lime or lemon. With these, I can create many easy yet delicious meals with the simplest of ingredients. I always try to use the best-quality ingredients for the best results, especially for fish sauce and soy sauce. Always buy a premium quality – it is simply not worth cutting corners on these staples.

ESSENTIAL INGREDIENTS

Something sweet
Sugar, honey, coconut syrup, palm sugar, rock sugar, fruit juices, maple syrup, agave nectar, fruit.

Something sour
Rice wine vinegar, cider vinegar, limes, lemons, yuzu, ponzu.

Something hot
Chillies, chilli sauce, chilli flakes, chilli oil, ginger root.

Something salty
Fish sauce, soy sauce, oyster sauce, mushroom sauce, sea salt.

Something umami
Fish sauce, hoisin sauce, seaweed, nuts, tahini, miso, oyster sauce, Marmite (or other yeast extract), mushroom, pork or chicken seasoning powder.

Cooking oils and other staples
I like to use a flavourless cooking oil, like vegetable, sunflower, groundnut (peanut) or refined rapeseed or olive oil for most of the cooking. It's also okay to use avocado or coconut oil if you have them. I also keep coconut milk, coconut water, sesame oil, teriyaki sauce, miso, rice, noodles, rice paper.

If you can only get five Vietnamese basics, you need: premium-quality fish sauce and soy sauce, rice and two kinds of noodles – rice and wheat. You can adapt flavours from lots of other ingredients listed to the left. You can get most of them from large supermarkets but there may be a few you need to source from Asian stores. You'll find readily available alternatives in the recipe notes.

A WORD ABOUT FISH SAUCE

Fish sauce is at the heart of Vietnamese cooking. It is made from fermented anchovies, so I tend to use fish sauce as an umami flavour in all my cooking especially with Italian. It mixes really well with garlic and butter for a lovely plain noodle dish with a vegetable or makes an excellent glaze with garlic, shallots, orange juice and honey on a roast. If you use it all the time, a bottle should serve a family of four for around 8 weeks. Just keep it in a cool, dark place and keep using it.

Most importantly ALWAYS use premium fish sauce. Always! It's available online and at Vietnamese supermarkets. It will make all the difference to your cooking, and will make everything you cook a real delight.

SOY SAUCES

Nothing beats a good soy, honey and lemon dressing for salads. You will always win over the crowds when you have a good dressing up your sleeve. Naturally brewed soy sauce is made from fermented soy beans, wheat and salt brine. There are many varieties and they will vary in saltiness, quality and taste.

Beware if you buy a Japanese one as it might be very salty and pair better with things like sushi. There are dark and light Chinese soy sauces, which can be confusing. Light soy sauce is mainly used for everyday cooking; it will flavour the food with more salt. If you use a thicker, dark soy sauce it will add more colour and a deeper, dominant flavour.

In Vietnamese cooking, people favour the Maggi brand, which is a hydrolyzed wheat protein sauce (wheat broken down with water) that was invented in Switzerland. It isn't really soy sauce, but it tastes like it and is always referred to as soy sauce.

SWEETNESS

Many of the recipes call for some sugar for the sweetness element. Caster (superfine) sugar is flavourless, cheap and dissolves easily, but you can use any type of sugar or sugar alternatives – I use honey, maple syrup, agave nectar and so on – as long as it adds the required sweetness. I also use rock sugar, which you will find in the world foods aisle at major supermarkets or Asian stores.

UNUSUAL HERBS AND GREENS

The recipes call for obtainable ingredients, but I do suggest a few more unusual ingredients for you to try if you can get hold of them. If not, don't worry, just leave them out or use greens and herbs you have access to and be guided by your taste buds. Coriander (cilantro) and mint are readily available. Here are a few suggested alternatives to give you some ideas.

List of Vietnamese herbs
Cockscomb, perilla (shiso), sawtooth, Vietnamese coriander (coriander) (laksa leaf), Thai basil, garlic chives, mugwort, a variety of assorted mints.

List of green & leafy vegetables
Chinese mustard leaves, broccoli leaves (kai lan), horseradish leaves, winter melon, Chinese cabbage (napa cabbage), snow pea shoots, pak choi, choi sum, water spinach/morning glory, Chinese celery leaves, chayotes.

MY KITCHEN TIPS

These are my tips from my kitchen to yours: ways to prepare swiftly, cook faster and make ahead.

It's always good to have an organised and clean kitchen before starting to cook. Whether you are cooking by heart or following a recipe, if your kitchen is organised, things are likely to flow better and your mind will be much clearer.

In this book, some of the recipes are quick and easy. Some traditional recipes, however, take some time and commitment, so if you are going to do those, you might as well do them properly. Make the most of your space so that it is a lovely place to cook in and you can take pleasure and delight in cooking.

TOOLS

You can cook a lot faster if you invest in a few simple tools to help you.

1. A sharp and reliable knife will make chopping and slicing really enjoyable and safe. I find a chef's knife indispensable for general everyday use.

2. A small, serrated knife is useful for small jobs, such as cutting soft fruit, vegetables, cake and bread.

3. A pair of kitchen scissors to cut herbs, vegetables and many other ingredients quickly can sometimes save you from using a chopping board.

4. There are a few jobs that food processors and hand blenders make easier, but on the whole I find that using a knife does the job and you don't need gadgets if you don't already have them.

5. A vegetable peeler. I always peel onions, shallots and garlic, as well as root vegetables, such as carrots, kohlrabi, daikon, parsnips and ginger root.

6. To help our environment, it is essential to compost food waste. Have a bowl on the counter to keep waste to hand and tip in the compost bin when it fills up.

7. I love my kettle. It's great for rehydrating rice noodles so you don't overcook them and to clean off raw meat, making cooking that little bit faster.

8. For thinly sliced vegetables and julienning, it's quick and useful to have a simple and reliable mandolin or a small julienne grater that are easy to wash.

9. At home, I have a stock pot and four saucepans in different sizes that are often used for everything from stock-making to egg-boiling.

10. The most essential small appliance is a rice cooker. If you love Vietnamese (and other Asian) food, you need this; there is no doubt that it will be the most used appliance you'll ever buy.

11. I have invested in a selection of lidded glass containers in different sizes so that I don't need to use cling film (plastic wrap) to store food and leftovers.

12. A simple and cheap bamboo steamer can help to re-heat leftovers and make various recipes with ease.

COOKING AND PREPARATION

Read each recipe from start to finish so that there are no surprises.
Prep all the ingredients ahead of time or use the cooking time to carry
on assembling bowls, and preparing sauces and additional ingredients.
Wash, peel, slice and chop anything that needs doing before cooking very
quick recipes so that nothing gets overcooked or burnt. This is the fastest
way to cook.

You can use a large plate to arrange the prepped ingredients, starting
at 12 o'clock for the first ingredient, then 1 o'clock for the next and so
on. I tend to slice up the vegetables first, starting with the driest to keep
my chopping board clean. Then I go for wet things, and then lastly the
meat or fish on another board. If certain recipes are house favourites,
always make extra and keep in the fridge for the next few days (or freeze)
because it can easily save you from cooking another meal. This works
really well with some one-pot recipes in the Ăn Cơm – Things to Eat
With Rice chapter, e.g. curry, braised pots as well as noodle soup broths.

MAKE AHEAD

I like to cook – vegetables, especially – as fresh as possible on the day
but many things can be made quite a way in advance to fit in with your
schedule, so use the storage times I have put on the recipes so you know
how long things will keep in the fridge. Be aware that although you can
make broths in advance, their delicate flavour will fade as the days pass;
add some extra spice or ingredients to boost flavour when you reheat.
You can make sauces and prepare rice and noodles earlier in the day.

Soak, wash and dry herbs with a salad spinner or lay on a tea towel
(dish towel) – keep in an airtight container ready to use and they keep
for longer.

Prepping ahead makes dinner parties a lot easier. Then you can
do the finishing touches – like the last-minute cooking of vegetables
so they stay nice and crunchy – before serving and spending time with
your guests.

I really enjoy cooking while listening to an audio book or *Desert
Island Discs*, or just quietly with my own meditations. When it's time
to serve and everyone is around, I like to be there too. I plan my time
around meals so that I don't need to rush and can spend time with
my loved ones. Vietnamese food lends itself really well to making ahead.
For example, I can put a Braised Pork Belly (page 26) or Caramelised
Hake (page 38) on the stove to cook in the morning so that we can
eat it in the evening for dinner. (It gets better with time.)

MY KITCHEN TIPS

1 ĂN CƠM – THINGS TO EAT WITH RICE

very day, families share an array of simple (to cook) dishes and eat together; they call this '*ăn cơm*' – which literally translates as 'eat rice'. Vietnamese people love to use an abundance of herbs and vegetables in everything and consider everyday food to be frugal and modest. There is usually a hot and invigorating broth with leafy greens at the table with glorious, freshly cooked vegetables. It is paired with the star of the show: mouth-watering and succulent fish or meat dishes that sit centre stage. Bowls of plain steamed rice and chopsticks are gathered together with sweet, sour, hot dipping sauces and pickles.

This food and way of eating always remind me of my family, even those young childhood memories stream through the flavours. I loved my mother's mother, who had a round, beaming face. I always remember her smiling; the crow's feet under her eyes were so deep the scorching south Vietnam sun couldn't reach their depths.

She would wash herbs grown in her garden and cleaver fish on a wooden stub under the shade of a jackfruit tree for a sweet and sour fish soup. She bought the fish from a sun-drenched fisherman at the beach as he came onto shore. She picked tomatoes from the vine next to a young mango tree she was nursing.

In the backdrop, a green, rusty American war tank sat abandoned in the shrubs with an after growth of pink and yellow flowers. After the war, the Vietnamese people suffered greatly from poverty and starvation. Despite these tragic memories, I will always remember my grandmother's smile in her eyes as she handed me a shell of coconut water. She would sweep the floor inside the house with a broom made from bamboo, the dust rising upwards against the light and floating out slowly. In an instant, lunch was ready – bowls of steamed rice clunked on the floor. Everyone at home gathered their squeaky, freshly washed feet onto the shiny ceramic floor, sitting cross-legged as the electric fan whipped itself around overhead, making a low woo-ing helicopter sound.

Before serving herself, my grandmother picked at the fish with her wooden chopsticks, dipped it onto the fish sauce and placed it into my bowl. She kept doing this because that's what you do – always give to those you love first. I would eat and eat to my heart's content. '*Ăn đi*,' she would say, '*go on, eat!*' My favourite meals are usually like that. A fish, pan-fried slowly so that its skin is crispy, served with a plate of crushed bird's eye chillies swimming in good fish sauce for dipping, steamed rice and a plate of vegetables. When ready, the soup is ladled into your rice bowl. Bringing it to your mouth you drink towards the end of the rice bowl to scoop up all the grains, ready for the next bowl.

SLOW-COOKED BEEF WITH LEMONGRASS, STAR ANISE & ROOT VEGETABLES

BÒ KHO

This recipe is reminiscent of beef *phở*. It's really comforting and bursting with brilliant, zesty flavours and soothing texture. I imagine it is very similar to a French *pot-au-feu* with lemongrass. I've used the traditional carrot and potatoes here, but you can replace them with a selection of root vegetables, such as swede, turnip and parsnip. It's really great with flat rice noodles or with rice, consumed on chilly evenings and even better for breakfast the next day with a baguette (pages 114–117).

Serves 4

2 tbsp vegetable oil
450 g (1 lb) grass-fed, free-range beef short rib, boned, cut into bite-sized cubes
1 onion, roughly chopped
2 celery stalks, sliced 1 cm (1.2 in) thick
15 g (½ oz) ginger root, finely chopped
2 lemongrass stalks, finely chopped
2 garlic cloves, sliced
1 tsp ground coriander
1 tsp ground cumin
4 whole cloves
8 star anise
1 cinnamon stick
300 ml (10 fl oz/1¼ cups) coconut water (or water)
300 ml (10 fl oz/1¼ cups) beef or chicken *phở* stock, beef stock or white wine
400 g (14 oz) potatoes, cut into chunks
300 g (10½ oz) carrots, sliced 2.5 cm (1 in) thick
1 tsp caster (superfine) sugar
2 tbsp fish sauce
60 g (2 oz) mangetout (snow peas)
chilli (hot pepper) flakes (optional)
freshly ground black pepper

For the garnish
lime or lemon wedges
Thai basil leaves
coriander (cilantro) leaves, roughly chopped

Heat a shallow, flameproof casserole dish (Dutch oven) over a high heat, add half the oil and brown off the beef on all sides for 2–3 minutes. Remove from the pan and set aside on paper towels. Reduce the heat to medium, add the remaining oil and fry off the onion, celery, ginger and lemongrass for about 5 minutes until soft, fragrant and slightly golden, then add the garlic. Return the beef to the pan with ground coriander and cumin. Mix well before pouring in the coconut water and stock. Add the cloves, star anise and cinnamon, cover and simmer gently for 2 hours.

Add the potatoes and carrots, season with sugar and fish sauce, cover and cook for a further 15 minutes over a low heat until the meat is cooked through and tender but still with some bite to it.

When ready to serve, bring the stew to the boil, stir in the mangetout and cook for 5 minutes. Season again with black pepper and chilli flakes to taste, if using. Serve with a squeeze of lime or lemon and a generous garnish of Thai basil or coriander.

Note • You can take this to the frying stage, then tip it into a slow or pressure cooker.

Make ahead   Cook: 5 days
Noodles, baguettes, herbs:
Same day

STICKY MUSTARD & MARMALADE RIBS

SƯỜN NƯỚNG SỐT MARMALADE

Anything on the bone is greatly appreciated and it is befitting to be seen tearing at ribs, licking your fingers and eating up every last morsel. It's very uncivilised to leave any meat on the bone, which is a waste. Ribs make a great meal and this easy in-the-storecupboard recipe hits the spot. It's one of my go-to recipes when I want to please a crowd as an addition to a feast or have one night for dinner with rice and poached vegetables. You can make this spicier by adding chilli sauce or chilli (hot pepper) flakes.

Serves 4

1.5 kg (3 lb 5 oz) free-range rack of pork ribs,
   or sliced into individual pieces, at room
   temperature
2 tsp garlic powder
5 tbsp soy sauce
5 tsp English mustard
2 heaped tbsp marmalade

Preheat the oven to 200°C (400°F/gas 8).

In a small bowl, mix together the garlic powder, 4 tablespoons of the soy sauce and the English mustard. Put the ribs in a lined baking tray, spoon over the marinade, turning so they are covered on all sides. Leave to sit for at least 20 minutes at room temperature (or overnight in the fridge). Turn the ribs to evenly distribute the marinade.

Bake in the oven, turning and basting occasionally for 45–50 minutes or until the juices run clear.

Meanwhile, combine the remaining soy sauce with the marmalade. Remove the ribs from the oven and brush with the marmalade sauce. Continue to bake for a further 5–8 minutes or until golden and slightly charred at the edges.

They are delicious hot or at room temperature served with sticky rice (page 199) or steamed rice (page 195).

Make ahead   Prep: Night before
               Cook: Serve immediately

BRAISED PORK BELLY & EGGS IN COCONUT WATER

THỊT KHO TÀU

Vietnamese people really like traditional *kho* dishes. It is a technique which means to braise, poach, steam and slow-cook meat, fish, tofu or vegetables all together in one – traditionally clay – pot. It's easy, efficient and makes for some really flavoursome dishes. *Kho* foods are comforting and will remind a lot of Vietnamese of home and of eating with their parents from childhood to adulthood. This dish is usually cooked with having leftovers in mind, especially as the flavour improves after a few days, so it's ideal to keep in the fridge and enjoy later.

Serves 4–6

1 kg (2 lb 4 oz) free-range pork belly or boneless pork leg, sliced into 2.5 cm (1 in) chunks, with fat and skin
3 round shallots, chopped
4–5 garlic cloves, finely chopped
½ tsp sea salt
½ tsp freshly ground black pepper, plus more to taste
3 tbsp vegetable oil
2 tbsp caster (superfine) sugar
600 ml (920 fl oz/2½ cups) coconut juice or water
4–6 eggs or 12 quail eggs or a mixture
4 bird's eye chillies, whole
5–6 tbsp fish sauce
1 tbsp coconut syrup or sugar for seasoning

Put the pork pieces in a bowl. Mix together the shallots, garlic, salt and pepper, add to the bowl and mix together well.

Heat the oil in a medium saucepan over a medium heat and sprinkle the sugar evenly over the surface of the pan. Watch over the pan for the sugar to caramelise. Resist the urge to stir. It should take 3½–4 minutes. Don't walk away or it will burn. As soon it becomes a golden colour, watch for it to slightly darken, then quickly add the pork to brown off. Let it sit for a minute, then stir, repeating until all sides are coloured.

Pour the coconut juice or water over the pork, cover and bring to a gentle simmer. Skim off any scum.

Meanwhile hard-boil and peel the eggs, then add them to the pan with the whole chillies and black pepper. Cover and simmer over a low heat for at least 2 hours, stirring occasionally. Season to taste with fish sauce, coconut syrup or sugar and more black pepper and cook for a further 15 minutes.

Serve with steamed rice (page 195) and plenty of vegetables.

Notes
- If you don't have coconut water, use water, adding sweetness to taste. You can also use cider or lemonade.
- You don't have to use a clay pot, but it's worth using one if you can as it provides more flavour.
- It's fine to use a leaner cut of meat.

Make ahead
Cook: 5 days
Rice: Same day

BAKED GINGER & LEMON CHICKEN

GÀ NƯỚNG

One of my favourite midweek meals takes minutes to prepare; sometimes, things just have to be that simple. Sultry ginger, tangy lemon, hot chillies and sticky honey are a great combo and you should have a supply of them in the kitchen to turn simple chicken into something rather special for those lazy, cosy evenings. You can also use chicken wings or pork ribs, but the cooking times will vary.

Serves 4

1 tbsp chilli (hot pepper) flakes, hotness of your
    choice (optional)
2.5 cm (1 in) ginger root, finely chopped
6 tbsp soy sauce
1 kg (2 lb 4 oz) skin-on chicken thighs and
    drumsticks
2 red onions, quartered
1 lemon, zested then sliced into rings
1 tbsp butter
2 tbsp clear honey

To serve
Steamed Rice (page 195)
selection of greens, like kale, broccoli
    and fine green beans
1 tbsp butter
½ tbsp vegetable oil
1 shallot, sliced
3 garlic cloves, sliced

Preheat the oven to 200°C (400°F/gas 8).

In a small bowl, mix together the dried chillies, if using, with the ginger and soy sauce, then coat the chicken pieces in the marinade in a roasting pan large enough not to crowd the chicken pieces; they should have a two-finger width space between them. Add the onion quarters, then arrange the lemon slices in between the pieces of chicken. Roast for 35 minutes, basting halfway through, until the chicken is tender.

Meanwhile, cook the rice and prepare a selection of greens.

After 35 minutes, take out the chicken, pour any juices into a small saucepan, then return the chicken to the oven.

Add the butter to the saucepan with the honey and lemon zest. Reduce for a few minutes until it has reduced by a third.

Take the chicken back out and pour the honey sauce evenly over the chicken, then cook for a further 5–10 minutes, or until the juices run clear when pierced at the thickest point. Remove from the oven and leave to rest for 5 minutes before serving.

Heat the oil in a medium saucepan over a medium heat and fry off the shallots until golden. Add the garlic, stirring to keep it from burning, then add the sliced vegetables to fry off with a splash of water to help it cook. Season with salt and pepper. Stir-fry for about 5 minutes.

Serve with an option of more dried chillies or chilli oil, steamed rice and vegetables.

Make ahead   Prep: Night before
                     Cook: Serve immediately

CHICKEN CURRY WITH SQUASH

CÀ RI GÀ BÍ

This is a mild, slurpy curry, meant to be dipped and mopped up with crispy Vietnamese baguettes or steamed rice. You can add different vegetables to the curry towards the end of cooking, depending on what's in season. Even frozen peas, cooked for a couple of minutes at the end, are a delight. You can also use chicken breast. As with most Vietnamese food, make it as hot as you like and feel free to add fresh chilli or chilli flakes to the curry.

Serves 3–4

40 g (1½ oz) ginger root, roughly chopped
2 lemongrass stalks, finely chopped
4 garlic cloves
2 tbsp vegetable oil
2 round shallots, roughly diced
500–600 g (1 lb 2 oz–1 lb 6 oz) chicken thighs, de-boned and excess fat removed, skin on, cut into large bite-sized pieces
3 tsp Vietnamese or mild curry powder
400 ml (13 fl oz/generous 1½ cups) coconut milk
100 ml (2½ fl oz/scant ½ cup) water
1 chicken stock cube
400 g (14 oz) potatoes, cut into 2 cm (¾ in) cubes
600 g (1 lb 5 oz) Delica squash, cut into 4 cm (1½ in) chunks
50 g (2 oz) mangetout (snow peas), sliced, or green garden peas (optional)
1½ tbsp fish sauce
1 tsp caster (superfine) sugar or maple syrup
freshly ground black pepper

For the garnish
15 g (½ oz) Thai basil or coriander (cilantro) leaves
2 spring onions (scallions), thinly sliced
2 fresh red chillies (optional)
½ lime

Using a hand blender or mortar and pestle, blend the ginger, lemongrass and garlic together with a tiny splash of water until smooth.

Heat the oil in a large saucepan or shallow casserole dish (Dutch oven) over a medium–high heat and cook the shallots until golden, then add the chicken to brown off for a couple minutes on each side. Add the garlic, ginger and lemongrass mixture and stir to combine.

Evenly sprinkle over the curry powder, stirring well to coat the chicken. Then add coconut milk, water and chicken stock cube, bring to a gentle boil, then add the potatoes and squash and stir to combine. Turn down the heat to low, cover and continue to simmer for about 15–20 minutes, or until the potatoes are soft.

Add the mangetout or peas. Season the curry with the fish sauce, sugar and a good pinch of black pepper and cook for a further 8–10 minutes.

Garnish with Thai basil and/or coriander, spring onions and red chillies, if using. Squeeze over some fresh lime juice.

Serve with steamed rice (page 195) or I like it best with a fresh baguette (pages 114–117) and butter.

GINGER CHICKEN

GÀ KHO GỪNG

Another classic *kho* recipe to do ahead and eat with rice. You can substitute the ginger with two stalks of finely chopped lemongrass or lime leaves. Reduce until it is sticky and caramelised, then enjoy with steamed or sticky rice. You can also use whole drumsticks and thighs, too; if you don't want to remove the bones, just cook it for a bit longer.

Serves 2

1½ tbsp vegetable oil or coconut oil
2 round shallots, roughly sliced
4 garlic cloves, finely chopped
3 tsp brown sugar
400 g (14 oz) chicken thighs, bones removed, skin on, sliced into bite-sized pieces
70 g (2½ oz) ginger root, julienned
150 ml (5 fl oz/scant ⅔ cup) coconut water
2–4 bird's eye chillies, whole
2 tbsp fish sauce
1 tsp heaped black pepper

For the garnish
spring onions (scallions), sliced lengthways and soaked in cold water until curled (optional)

Heat ½ tablespoon of the oil over a gentle heat in a saucepan that will fit the chicken pieces snuggly. Fry the shallots until golden, then add the garlic. Stay and watch over the pan until the garlic turns golden, then remove the shallots and garlic from the pan, leaving any oil, and set aside in a small bowl.

Add the remaining oil to the same pan and increase the heat to medium. Spread the brown sugar evenly over the surface of the pan. Watch over the pan for the sugar to caramelise, resisting the urge to stir. It should take 3½–4 minutes, but don't take your eyes off it as it will burn very quickly. As soon it becomes a golden colour, watch for it to slightly darken, then immediately add the chicken pieces and let them sizzle away for a couple of minutes before turning. Add the ginger, let it sit for 2 minutes, then add the coconut water. Return the fried shallot and garlic to the pan with the bird's eye chillies, fish sauce and black pepper.

Cover and cook over a low heat for 10 minutes, then remove the lid to reduce for a further 10–15 minutes. It should be reduced and quite succulent and sticky.

When ready to serve, garnish with spring onions. Serve with rice and plenty of greens.

Make ahead   Cook: 3 days
              Rice: Same day

HAINAN CHICKEN & RICE

CƠM GÀ HẢI NAM

Vietnamese food can be very vibrant and colourful as well as basic and simple. This chicken and rice recipe evokes the essential feeling of home and pure comfort. It's even okay eaten in silence, for that quietness from everyone around the table denotes contentedness. Adopted from Hainan island's most famous dish, this unbeatable staple is imbued with an abundance of vivid flavours and furnished with an array of sauces, leaves and vegetables. It is quite involved considering how simple it is, but this has to be done right or not at all.

Serves 3–4

For the poached chicken
1.5 kg (3 lb 5 oz) free-range, organic, corn-fed
    chicken (French, if possible)
2 tbsp sea salt
2.5 litres (88 fl oz/10 cups) water
50 g (2 oz) ginger root, sliced
3 pandan leaves, tied into small knots (if you can't
    get hold of these, don't let that stop you)

For the ginger & spring onion sauce
2 tbsp groundnut (peanut) oil or avocado oil
50 g (2 oz) ginger root, grated
1 garlic clove, grated
3 spring onions (scallions), green and white parts,
    sliced 1 cm (¾ in) thick
pinch of sea salt
1 tsp caster (superfine) sugar

For the soy dipping sauce
4 tbsp soy sauce
1 tbsp maple syrup
2 tsp sesame oil
1 tbsp rice wine vinegar
100 ml (2½ fl oz/scant ½ cup) chicken stock from
    poaching chicken, hot

For the chilli-garlic sauce
4 red bird's eye chillies
80 g (3 oz) ginger root, sliced
4 garlic cloves
2 tsp caster (superfine) sugar
½ tsp sea salt
1 juice of lime
2 tbsp rendered chicken fat (or other fat)
80 ml (2½ fl oz/scant ⅓ cup) chicken stock from
    poaching the chicken

For the chicken rice

300 g (10½ oz) jasmine rice
3 tbsp chicken fat
1 round shallot, roughly sliced
20 g (¾ oz) ginger root, sliced
500 ml (17 fl oz/2 cups) chicken broth
5 garlic cloves, left whole
1 heaped tsp turmeric
1 tsp mushroom or chicken powder (optional)
1 tsp sea salt

For the chicken broth

chicken broth from poaching the chicken
1 spring onion (scallion), sliced diagonally 5 mm
    (¼ in) thick
20 g (¾ oz) coriander (cilantro) leaves,
    coarsely chopped
freshly ground black pepper

For the garnish

1 cucumber, sliced
¼ bunch coriander (cilantro) leaves and stalks
handful of Vietnamese coriander (cilantro) leaves
variety of tomatoes, sliced into quarters or rings

First, poach the chicken. Trim off and set aside any excess fat from the opening of the cavity and around the neck of the chicken. Rub 1 tablespoon of sea salt onto the chicken to exfoliate the skin, (which will give it a shiny, smooth sheen), going around the thighs, wings, back and front. To give the chicken skin a firm and springy texture later on, place the chicken in a pan, pour boiling water over it, then leave for 5 minutes. Then drain, discard water and carefully rinse off in the sink with slow-running cold water. Wash the pan and clean down your sink and surface areas.

In the same pan, bring the measured water to the boil. Then add the chicken, 1 tablespoon of sea salt, the ginger and the pandan knots. Return to the boil, then reduce to a simmer, cover and cook over a low heat for 40 minutes. Turn off the heat and leave the chicken to sit, without removing the lid, for 25 minutes.

Meanwhile, place the chicken fat into a frying pan (skillet) over a medium–high heat and render the chicken fat for a few minutes. Even if you only have a little bit, it's worth doing to add flavour. Leave in the pan and set aside.

In another small frying pan, make the ginger and spring onion sauce by combining all the ingredients together and gently fry on low heat for 5 minutes until soft, then place in a bowl and set aside.

Next, make the soy dipping sauce by combining all the ingredients except the chicken broth together in a large jar.

To make the chilli-garlic sauce, blend the chillies, ginger and garlic to paste in a mini chopper/blender or finely chop, then pound together in a mortar and pestle with the sugar, salt and lime juice. Add the hot rendered chicken fat or hot oil. When the chicken is cooked, add the broth and stir well together.

When the time is up, take the chicken out of the cooking pan, reserving the broth and transfer into an ice-cold water bath. Leave it there for 10 minutes, then drain and leave to rest.

Meanwhile, wash the rice three times, then drain. Heat the chicken fat in the frying pan over a medium heat, add the shallots and ginger and fry until golden, then add the rice. Mix well for a couple of minutes, then add to a rice cooker with 500 ml (17 fl oz/2 cups) of the chicken broth and the rest of the ingredients. Stir together and cook in a rice cooker.

If you don't have a rice cooker, cook the rice in a saucepan over a low heat with the lid on. When the broth has seeped into the rice, stir well and continue to cook over a low heat with the lid still firmly on to let the steam do its work for a further 15–18 minutes still without removing the lid. Take off the heat and let it rest for 5–10 minutes. Then fluff up the rice with a spoon.

When the chicken has cooled, separate the meat from the carcass with a sharp knife, keeping the skin intact. I like to start with the thighs by separating them from the cavity and cutting at the joints. To separate the breast, I like to score right down the middle of the two and dissect it from there, slicing along its sides and wings. To separate the meat from the leg bones, move the knife along the bones. Slice the meat up against the grain, 1 cm thick, with the skin still intact and display on a serving plate. Garnish with cucumber slices, sprigs of coriander and a variety of seasonal tomatoes.

When ready to serve, warm the reserved chicken broth to add to the dipping sauce and the chilli-garlic sauce. Combine and serve in separate dipping sauce bowls. Add the remaining broth to soup bowls with spring onion, coriander and black pepper.

Serve the chicken and rice with an array of vegetable side dishes to make a luscious feast.

Make ahead   Sauces: Day before
Cook: Same day

CARAMELISED HAKE WITH FISH SAUCE & GINGER

CÁ KHO TỘ

This is a staple Vietnamese *kho* dish, typical in so many households and traditionally eaten together with rice, plenty of pickles and vegetables. It can be adapted in all sorts of ways depending on what type of fish you use and what you add to the pot. Here, it's with ginger, but you can use lemongrass or just shallots or garlic. You can make this quite brothy (to flavour the rice) but it is also exquisite when it's sticky and caramelised. The dish keeps really well; it's a great make-ahead meal. Place the fish in the middle next to bowls of fresh rice for each person to take a little at a time.

Serves 2

3 tbsp vegetable oil
1 small round Asian shallot, diced
20 g (¾ oz) ginger root, finely chopped
3 garlic cloves, finely chopped
1 tbsp caster (superfine) sugar for the caramel,
    plus 1 tbsp extra to season
2 x 300 g (11 oz) hake steaks
75 ml (2½ fl oz/scant ⅓ cup) coconut water
    or water
2 tbsp fish sauce
2 bird's eye chillies, whole
½ tsp black pepper

For the garnish
1 spring onion (scallion), sliced diagonally
    1 cm (½ in) thick
10 g (½ oz) ginger root, julienned

Heat 1 tablespoon of the oil over a low heat in a saucepan that will fit the fish snuggly. Add the shallot and ginger and cook until golden, then add the garlic. Watch over the pan until the garlic turns golden, then remove from the pan and set aside in a small bowl.

Add the remaining oil to the same pan over a medium heat, then sprinkle the sugar evenly over the surface of the pan. Watch over the pan for the sugar to caramelise. Resist the urge to stir. It should take 3½–4 minutes. Don't walk away or it will burn. As soon it becomes a golden colour, watch for it to slightly darken, then add the fish steaks immediately, flesh-side down. Let them sit for a few minutes, then add the coconut water, fish sauce and extra sugar. Add the fried shallot, ginger and garlic back to pan, then the whole bird's eye chillies and plenty of black pepper. Cover and cook over a low heat for 20–30 minutes. Remove the lid and simmer for another 5 minutes to reduce the sauce further.

When ready to serve, garnish with spring onions and ginger root. Serve with rice and plenty of greens.

Notes	◆ Use any sustainably caught fish. Get your fishmonger to cut the fish into steaks.
	◆ Avoid fish with small bones as the flesh will flake easily, and be fiddly to eat.
Make ahead	Cook: 3 days Rice: Same day

SEA BASS IN TOMATO, CELERY & DILL BROTH

CANH CHUA LÁ THÌ LÀ

This is one of my most favourite traditional meals that I love sharing with my mum and Olive. This is a classic, easy, one-pot wonder – and my mum makes the best version. Known as 'sour soup', *canh chua* is loved by our family and all Vietnamese people because of its perfect balance of sweet, sour and hot tanginess. It cleverly makes two dishes in one – a fish broth, which is spooned onto plates and served with the fish that flavoured the soup.

Everybody at the table should share small morsels of fish at a time, dipping in the pool of spicy fish sauce and ladling the soup into their rice bowls whenever they wish. It is really important to prepare all the ingredients before you begin the cooking process, then you can cook everything quickly. Make sure the rice is cooked beforehand.

Serves 2

1 sea bass, cleaned (ask fishmonger to slice
    into 1 in steaks including head and tail
    (about 4) with bones)
1 tbsp vegetable oil
2 round shallots, sliced
1 garlic clove, finely chopped
1 litre (34 fl oz/4 cups) homemade or good-quality
    chicken or pork stock (or boiling water)
1 celery stalk, sliced into 5 cm (2 in) at a diagonal,
    plus a handful of leaves for garnishing
2 tomatoes, cut into bite-sized chunks
1 tbsp caster (superfine) sugar
4 tbsp fish sauce
1 juice of lime
30 g (1 oz) dill fronds, sliced into 1 cm (½ in) lengths
1 spring onion (scallion), sliced
freshly chopped chillies (optional)

For the dipping sauce
1–2 bird's eye chillies
3 tbsp fish sauce

Heat a small pan on a medium heat, fry the sliced shallots gently until golden in 1 tablespoon of oil, stirring occasionally, then add the garlic. Watch until the garlic turns golden then set aside.

Pour the chicken or pork stock (or boiling water) into a pot, add tomatoes, sugar and fish sauce, and cover with a lid. Let this come to the boil then immediately add the sea bass chunks, including head and tail. Cover.

When this reaches a boil, bring the heat down to simmer for about 3–5 minutes, depending on the size of your fish. Then add the spring onion, celery stalk, fried shallot and garlic, including their oil, and the lime juice. Taste to adjust the sweet, sour and salty balance, adding more sugar if a little more sweetness is needed, more lime for sour and more fish sauce for umami. To check if the fish is cooked, pierce a knife through the deepest part – if it reaches the bone easily it is cooked.

Make the sauce on a plate large enough to hold a couple of the fish steaks. Crush the bird's eye chillies with the back of a spoon onto the plate, then add the fish sauce. Take out a couple of fish steaks and place onto the plate with the sauce. Then put the rest of the soup into a large serving bowl for the middle of the table. Garnish with celery leaves and dill.

Notes
• Substitute the sea bass for cod,
  haddock, monkfish, carp, prawns,
  scallop or razor clams.
• Instead of dill, you can use
  coriander (cilantro) or mint.
• If you don't have chicken stock,
  use water and a stock cube.

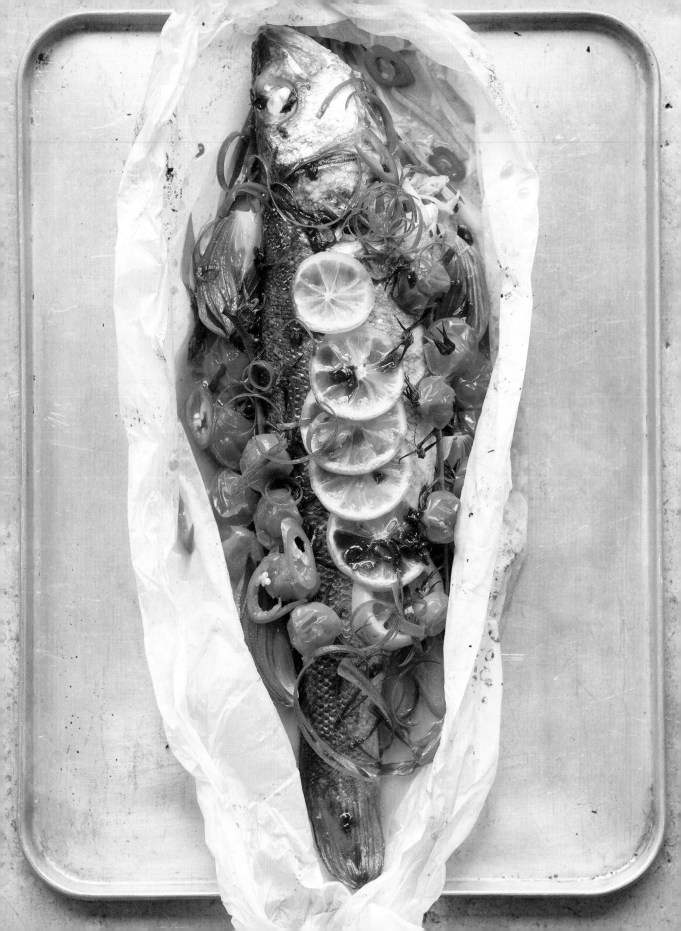

SEA BASS PARCELS WITH GINGER & KIMCHI

CÁ SEABASS NƯỚNG BAO GIẤY

This recipe is typical of the ingredients I always have in my kitchen, but you can adapt it to yours. Steaming the parcel in the oven is quick and easy. I love opening this at the table when you have a guest or two and hearing the ooohs and ahhhs as though I am opening a gift. For dinner parties, wrap more parcels and bake together, increasing the cooking times.

Serves 2–4, depending if you want a whole fish to yourself

1 tbsp vegetable oil
1 x 800 g (1 lb 12 oz) sea bass or 2 x 400 g (12 oz) sea bass, cleaned, gutted, scaled, head on
40 g (1½ oz) ginger root, julienned
2 tbsp kimchi, sliced 1 cm (¾ in) thick
1 lemon, zested then sliced into rings
2 red onions, quartered
2 stems of cherry tomatoes on the vine
½ tbsp sesame oil
80 ml (2½ fl oz/scant ⅓ cup) coconut water or fish or chicken stock

For the dressing
1 tsp vegetable oil
2 spring onions (scallions), white and green parts, sliced 1 cm (½ in) thick
4–5 tbsp soy sauce, depending on the size of the fish
1 tbsp cider vinegar
1 tbsp caster (superfine) sugar
1 tbsp chilli sauce
1 spring onion (scallion), thinly sliced lengthways, soaked in cold water until curled
1 red chilli, sliced diagonally 5 mm (¼ in) thick

Preheat the oven to 180°C (350°F/gas 4).

Place a sheet of parchment paper large enough to wrap a fish on a baking dish. Drizzle a ½ tablespoon of the vegetable oil on the surface of the paper, place the fish onto it and stuff the neck opening with the ginger and the body of the fish with the kimchi. Place the lemon rings on the skin and scatter onion quarters and cherry tomatoes around the fish. Pour over the coconut water or stock. Drizzle over the sesame oil on the fish then wrap *en papillotte* style (sealing any openings) and bake for 35 minutes.

Meanwhile, prepare the dressing. Heat the oil in a saucepan over a medium heat and fry the spring onions for about a minute. Then add the soy sauce, cider vinegar, sugar and chilli sauce, mixing well, and bring to a gentle boil.

Once the fish is cooked, I usually take it to the table and unwrap it there, pouring the hot dressing over it, then garnishing with curly lengths of spring onion and red chillies.

Serve with steamed rice (page 195) and plenty of greens and a refreshing soup.

Notes
• If you don't have kimchi, just leave it out.

Make ahead
Prep: Night before
Cook: Serve immediately

FRIED BRILL ON WATERCRESS WITH A CHILLI-LIME SWEET & SOUR SAUCE

CÁ CHIÊN NƯỚC MẮM CHUA NGỌT CẢI XÀ LÁCH XOONG

Sitting down to share a fried brill at lunch or dinner (*ăn cơm*) is a simple comforting pleasure for all Vietnamese people. Break off a small chunk, take it to your rice bowl and eat with vegetables and pickles. In Vietnam, it's considered uncouth to take a big chunk from the dish. Rather, it's all about sharing and giving the best bits to younger kids or the elderly.

Serves 2–4, depending on the size of the fish

3 tbsp vegetable oil
1 brill, cleaned and head removed, patted dry
    with paper towel
6 lime leaves
250 g (9 oz) watercress

For the sauce
2 tbsp lime juice
zest of 1 lime
2 tbsp caster (superfine) sugar
2 tbsp fish sauce
2 garlic cloves, finely chopped
1 bird's eye chilli, finely chopped

Heat the oil in a frying pan (skillet) big enough to fit your fish over a low–medium heat. Add the fish and lime leaves and shallow-fry for 7–10 minutes on each side or until golden and crisp.

Meanwhile, prepare the sauce by combining all the ingredients together.

When the fish is cooked, place it on a big plate surrounded by the fresh watercress. Pour over the sauce and serve immediately. Serve with steamed rice (page 195), a soup and plenty of vegetables and pickles.

Notes
- Use any sustainably sourced whole fish.
- You can also quickly pan fry fillets until golden.
- Substitute the watercress with sliced white cabbage, a crunchy sliced vegetable salad, unripe mango or green papaya. However, if you have no vegetables at all, it is still SO good.

Make ahead
Sauce: Day before
Cook: Serve immediately

OMELETTE WITH CARROT, CABBAGE & CHINESE SAUSAGE

TRỨNG CHIÊN CÀ RỐT BẮP CẢI & LẠP XƯỞNG

On days when there simply isn't time or you don't have the energy to cook, these 5-minute dishes make a delightful and satisfying meal. Stuff it in a lovely fresh *bánh mì* (page 114) or put on some rice in the rice cooker and create a quick meal with eggs. Add herbs or vegetables to top it off. This is a great recipe to use up the leftovers of fresh ingredients you have laying around.

Serves 1

2 eggs, beaten
¼ tsp caster (superfine) sugar
2 tsp soy sauce
freshly ground black pepper
1 Chinese sausage (*lạp xưởng*), sliced into 3 mm (⅛ in) rings
1 large garlic clove, finely chopped
1 round shallot or spring onion (scallion), sliced
¼ carrot, julienned
20 g (¾ oz) flat head or white cabbage, thinly sliced
4 coriander (cilantro) stems, roughly chopped
15 g (½ oz) garlic chives, sliced into 3 cm (1 in) pieces

Mix together the eggs, sugar, soy sauce and pepper. Set a frying pan (skillet) over a medium heat, add the sausage pieces and let them sit in the pan for about 2–3 minutes until they start to sizzle and turn golden at the edges. Add the garlic, shallot or spring onion, carrot and cabbage and stir-fry for a few minutes. Then pour over the egg mixture and swivel the pan to spread it all over. Using chopsticks or a wooden spoon, push one side of the egg towards the centre of the pan and swivel the pan to cover the surface area with egg. Rotate the pan and push a couple more times until it is cooked on the base, then flip it over to cook for a further minute.

Note

• Use in a Bảnh Mí (page 114) with pickles, herbs, spring onion and cucumber.
• If you don't have Chinese sausage, use cured cuts of charcuterie or go meatless and add any crunchy julienned vegetables you have to hand.

Herbs and vegetables are just as important as fish or meat in a Vietnamese diet, simply because they make the entire meal complete and utterly delicious. Bringing freshness, texture and balance to every dish, vegetables are celebrated and eaten seasonally in abundance. Vegetables are expected at every meal whether they have been pickled, poached, fried or sliced. Plentiful herbs are treated like salad leaves and not decoration – texture and flavours of leaves create and bring dishes to life.

I have lived in London most of my life and I love British vegetables, and indeed British food, and those I have discovered all over the Western world. When I was growing up, my mother adapted British vegetables, like cauliflower, cabbages, spinach, watercress and asparagus with Vietnamese flavours – flash-fried with garlic or engulfed with a sweet and sour sauce, poached in a gingery soup or simply just blanched and dipped in a lovely sauce.

In this chapter, you'll find that the recipes are littered with vegetables that are unknown to the Vietnamese – like Jerusalem artichoke, samphire and asparagus – because here, they are readily available and adapt so well to the Vietnamese style of cooking. Enjoy runner beans, tenderstem broccoli, kale, cavolo nero and even *cime di rapa*, all given the Vietnamese treatment.

I like to use as much of every part of vegetables and herbs where appropriate. I freeze peels and skins for vegetable stocks to maximise flavour, save zest from squeezed lemons and limes where I can, and use stalks and the ends of herbs in soups. Sometimes I even re-root produce, such as spring onions, Vietnamese coriander (cilantro) and cockscomb stalks, in a glass of water and grow on the window sill.

TOFU PILLOWS, TOMATOES & BROCCOLI IN FISH SAUCE

TÀU HỦ XÀO BÔNG CẢI CÀ CHUA

When tofu is cooked properly, it is soft, pillowy and smooth – like bouncing on a cloud. It is absolutely delicious with just the sweetest summer tomatoes, but here I've added extra vegetables with different colours and textures making it a feast for the eyes and the belly. Use whatever you have to hand to make it special, even if it is just a Tuesday night.

Serves 2–3 as a side dish

For the tofu
2 tbsp vegetable oil
pinch of sea salt
400 g (14 oz) fresh firm tofu, cut into 3 x 4 cm
    (1 x 1½ in) pieces and patted dry

For the vegetables
1 round shallot, finely chopped
1 garlic clove, finely chopped
165 g (5½ oz) cherry tomatoes, halved
75 g (2½ oz) mushrooms of choice
100 g (3½ oz) tenderstem broccoli,
    cut into bite-sized florets
2 tbsp Shaoxing wine or mirin
1 tbsp fish sauce

For the garnish
3 spring onions (scallions), sliced diagonally
small handful of coriander (cilantro) leaves

Heat a large frying pan (skillet) or wok, add half the oil and a pinch of salt, then fry the tofu over a medium heat for about 8 minutes on each side until golden. Remove from the heat and lift the tofu out onto paper towels to soak off any excess oil.

Put the frying pan back over a medium–high heat, add the remaining oil and brown off the shallot, then add the garlic and fry until golden. Add the tomatoes and keep them still for a couple of minutes to brown, then gently turn. After about 4 minutes, add the mushrooms and broccoli and quickly stir-fry for a couple of minutes. Add the fried tofu, Shaoxing wine or mirin and fish sauce, gently stirring for another 2–3 minutes.

Garnish with the spring onions and coriander and serve with steamed rice (page 195) or vermicelli (page 202).

Notes
- Use soy sauce instead of fish sauce to make this dish vegan.
- If you want to make a bigger batch of tofu, you can store it in the fridge for a few days.

Make ahead
Tofu: 3–4 days
Cook: Serve immediately

RUNNER BEANS &
CELERY LEAVES WITH GARLIC

ĐẬU TÂY XÀO TỎI

Fresh and crunchy runner beans are great in the summer and easy to grow too. When buying celery, choose a leafy bunch as the leaves are entirely edible and have a surprisingly complex flavour that can bring real vigour to a dish – as they do in this one.

Serves 4 as a side dish

½ tbsp vegetable oil
3 garlic cloves, crushed
300 g (10½ oz) runner beans, strings removed and beans sliced lengthways
70 g (2½ oz) celery leaves (or more to taste)
1 tbsp oyster sauce
2 tbsp water
freshly ground black pepper (optional)
chilli oil (optional)
chilli (hot pepper) flakes (optional)
coriander (cilantro) leaves, chopped (optional)

Place the runner beans into a mixing bowl, pour over boiling water from a kettle to cover, then let them blanch for 2 minutes. Drain.

Heat the oil on a large frying pan (skillet) or wok over a medium heat, add the garlic and cook for a minute until golden. Immediately add the runner beans and celery leaves and stir-fry with the oyster sauce and water for about 3–5 minutes. Season, if you like, with black pepper, chilli oil, chilli flakes, coriander or extra celery leaves, then serve immediately on a platter.

Note
♦ Use fine green beans, broccoli, asparagus, okra (ladies' fingers) or other vegetables if you wish.

SAUTÉED MUSHROOMS & JERUSALEM ARTICHOKES

NẤM XÀO CỦ CÚC VU

I love fresh mushrooms in all their varieties and find that they take on the many flavours of Vietnamese sauces so well. Here, I am using non-typical shiso dressing and tahini, which you can purchase at Japanese stores, but you could use any of the sauces on pages 208–211. I love Jerusalem artichokes and find that they pair incredibly well with mushrooms. If they are out of season, try water chestnuts or radishes for the crunch and texture, which contrasts the soft and silky mushrooms.

Serves 2–4

1 tbsp tahini
1 tbsp soy sauce
1 tbsp store-bought shiso dressing (optional)
½ tbsp maple syrup
½ tbsp vegetable oil
10 cm (4 in) leek, sliced 5 mm (¼ in) thick
1 red chilli, sliced
10 g (½ oz) butter
2 garlic cloves, sliced
100 g (3½ oz) Jerusalem artichoke, sliced 3 mm
    (⅛ in) thick
300 g (10½ oz) various mushrooms, roughly sliced
30 g (1 oz) Vietnamese coriander (cilantro) leaves
¼ lime

Combine the tahini, soy sauce, shiso dressing, if using, and maple syrup in a small bowl. Set aside.

Heat the oil in a large frying pan (skillet) over a medium heat and fry the leek and chilli for 5 minutes. Add the butter and garlic and cook for 1 minute until golden. Turn the heat to high, add the Jerusalem artichoke and let it sit for a minute before stirring well, then adding the mushrooms. Stir-fry until the mushrooms are slightly wilted.

Pour the sauce all over the mushrooms and cook for a minute or so until they've wilted but still hold their shape. Remove from the heat and leave to cool for a few minutes. Mix in the coriander, then serve with wedges of lime to squeeze over the plate.

SOY AUBERGINES & THAI BASIL

CÀ TÍM XÀO NƯỚC TƯƠNG

This is real crowd pleaser. It's so good that you'd want to have it all to yourself over (*bánh hỏi*) noodles or enjoyed singularly with rice. You can make this as hot and spicy as you like. If you have guests, steam the aubergines and make the sauce in advance, then this only needs to be fried and garnished when you are ready to serve. I make this in a steamer but I have given instructions for those who don't have one.

You might need to cook in batches, depending on the size of your pan, so before you start cooking, assess the best way forward and have a warm plate ready for the first cooked batch.

Serves 3–4

30 g (1 oz) butter
2 round shallots, finely chopped
2 large red chillies, sliced
2 garlic cloves, thinly sliced
1 tsp sesame oil
2 aubergines (eggplants), cut into 2.5 cm
    (1 in) chunks
2 spring onions (scallions), thinly sliced
4 stems Thai basil, leaves only

For the sweet soy sauce
2 tbsp soy sauce
1 tsp cider vinegar
1 tbsp chilli sauce
1 garlic clove, finely chopped
3 tsp maple syrup
chilli oil (optional)

Place the aubergines in a boiling steamer for 5 minutes until tender – in batches, if necessary – or steam in a metal colander over a pan of boiling water.

Prepare the sauce by stirring all the ingredients in a bowl or shaking in a jar.

Use a very large wok or frying pan (skillet) or cook in batches to avoid over-crowding. Heat the wok or pan over a very high heat, add the butter, shallots, chillies and garlic and cook for about a minute. Add the sesame oil and the aubergine chunks and stir-fry for 3–4 minutes, charring the edges. Then pour over the prepared sauce and mix in all the spring onions and three-quarters of the Thai basil and continue to stir-fry for 1 minute. Garnish with the remaining Thai basil and add some hot chilli oil, if you wish.

Serve immediately as part of a sharing meal with steamed rice (page 195) or with a plate of rice vermicelli (bánh hỏi) or 0.8 mm rice vermicelli (bún) (page 202).

Notes
- If you don't have Thai basil, use coriander (cilantro) or sliced onions.
- Try this with all varieties of aubergines. I love the stripey purple ones, called graffiti.

KALE WITH SHALLOTS, GINGER, KIMCHI & ORZO

CẢI XOĂN XÀO GỪNG

This is a lovely mix of fresh vegetables and pickles combined. I've added orzo pasta to this to make more of a meal out of it – it's a great packed lunch – but you don't have to include it if it's part of a sharing rice meal.

Serves 4

50 g (2 oz) orzo
½ tbsp vegetable oil
2 round shallots, sliced
30 g (1 oz) ginger root, finely chopped
10 g (½ oz) butter
250 g (9 oz) summer kale varieties, sliced 2 cm (¾ in) thick
1 heaped tbsp kimchi, sliced 5 mm (¼ in) thick
pinch of sea salt and freshly ground black pepper

Start by cooking the orzo according to the packet instructions in water seasoned with some sea salt. Once cooked, reserve 75 ml (2½ fl oz/scant ⅓ cup) of the pasta water before draining.

On a medium heat in a large frying pan (skillet), add the oil, then the shallots and ginger and fry until golden then add the butter. Once it's melted, add the kale, stir-fry to wilt then ladle in some hot pasta water. Watch it sizzle for 30 seconds then combine with the kimchi and cooked orzo. Season with salt and pepper. Once the water has evaporated, it is ready to serve.

Note

- Other leaves to fry include: *cime di rapa*, mustard leaves, chard, beetroot leaves, turnip tops, Chinese cabbage, Savoy, sweetheart or white cabbage, Chinese broccoli, *choi sum*, morning glory – the list is endless.

FRIED WATERCRESS, PEA SHOOTS & TAHINI

XÀ LÁCH XOONG xào ĐỌT ĐẬU HOÀ LAN SỐT BƠ VỪNG

Watercress is such a gorgeous and versatile leaf to be enjoyed raw or cooked. I've added a few other greens to this as it wilts down a lot. If you can get hold of mugwort leaves, they're great with this recipe too.

Serves 2–4

1 tbsp tahini
2 tsp soy sauce
½ tbsp vegetable oil
2 garlic cloves, left whole
15 g (½ oz) dried seaweed, soaked in hot water
    for 10 minutes, then thinly sliced (optional)
300 g (10½ oz) watercress
handful of spinach leaves
handful of pea shoots
¼ lemon
freshly ground black pepper
8 raspberries, halved (optional)
pinch of Japanese ichimi chilli (hot pepper) flakes
    (optional)

In a small bowl, mix together the tahini and soy sauce. Heat the oil and garlic in a frying pan (skillet) over a medium heat and wait until it gets hot and the garlic is slightly charred, moving it around the pan to infuse the oil. Turn the heat to high. Add the seaweed, if using, and cook for 3 minutes.

Add the watercress to the pan. Pour over the tahini and soy sauce and stir-fry for 1 minute. Turn off the heat and fold in the spinach until it is nearly wilted. Place immediately onto a serving plate, garnish with pea shoots and squeeze fresh lemon juice over the top.

Season with black pepper, broken up raspberries and Japanese ichimi chilli flakes, if using.

Note
- You can use ordinary chilli (hot pepper) flakes if you can't get ichimi flakes, although you should find them in Asian stores.

64

HOT & FIERY GREENS WITH ANCHOVIES

CẢI XÀO ỚT CÁ CƠM

You need to get the pan really hot to create the loud and appetising sounds of steam, sizzle and colliding metal utensils clashing against a wok, followed by the lush aroma of buttery garlic and ginger.

You can use a variety of vegetables for this or just one kind; the garlic, ginger and anchovies will lift the vegetables to another level and you'll find that these vegetable sides become household favourites, making great additions to many meals. You can also use water or chicken stock instead of white wine. Change it up every time.

Serves 2–4

1 tbsp vegetable oil
30 g (1 oz) ginger root, julienned
1 Asian or small round shallot, sliced
2 red chillies, finely chopped
15 g (½ oz) butter
1 tsp fish sauce
4 garlic cloves, finely chopped
4–6 anchovies, coarsely chopped
50 g (2 oz) cavolo nero, sliced 3 cm (1 in) thick
100 g (3½ oz) baby courgettes (zucchini),
    halved lengthways
100 g (3½ oz) tenderstem broccoli, sliced diagonally
    3 cm (1 in) thick
100 g (3½ oz) fine green beans, topped and tailed
75 ml (2½ fl oz/⅓ cup) white wine

Have a wok or large frying pan (skillet) on a high heat to get it hot. Add the vegetable oil, ginger, shallot and chillies and cook for 2 minutes until lightly golden. Add the butter, fish sauce, garlic and anchovies – stir, fry and toss. Add the vegetables and let sit for 1 minute to char. Toss again, then leave to sit for another minute. Finally, add the white wine – if your pan is hot, this should create some flames. Leave to sit for a couple of minutes then cover with a lid for 1 minute. The vegetables should be soft but still retain some bite. Serve immediately.

SUMMER TOMATOES, CELERY LEAVES & THAI BASIL

CÀ CHUA MÙA HÈ

Tomatoes are usually served as they are without any dressing as an accompaniment to meals. But when the variety we can get in the summer months offers us the most beautiful flavours, shapes, colours and sizes, it's hard to resist the urge to create a meal out of them, complete with a dressing to celebrate the season. You can use what you have to hand in your storecupboard or fridge, just follow the balance to bring across the sweet, salty, sour, umami and hot flavours. It's also good with some torn leftover roast chicken or grilled prawns and served with extra fresh baguettes (pages 114–117), or piled on toasted garlic ciabatta.

Serves 4

For the dressing
1 tbsp fish sauce or soy sauce
1 tbsp maple syrup or honey
zest of 1 lime plus 1 tbsp juice
1 red chilli, sliced (optional)
2 tsp English mustard
¼ tsp freshly ground black pepper
1 tbsp pistachios or peanuts, chopped or blended

For the salad
1 red onion, thinly sliced
400 g (14 oz) various tomatoes, sliced into
    different-sized pieces
20 cm (8 in) baguette, torn into bite-sized pieces
2–3 Thai basil stalks or coriander (cilantro)
handful of celery leaves
Crispy Shallots (page 206)

Combine the dressing ingredients, mix or shake well together. Set aside. Toss the onions and tomatoes with the dressing. Add the toasted baguette chunks and garnish with Thai basil, celery leaves and crispy shallots.

CHAYOTES & GARLIC

CỦ SU XÀO TỎI

Chayotes are probably quite unknown in the West but I have started to see them pop up in a few places and wanted to feature them as they are so utterly gorgeous. They have the texture of apple but taste refreshing, like a hybrid of mild pear and radish. They are really crunchy and take on garlic beautifully. I love chayotes just like this – plain and simple. The dish goes really well and will prove popular as a vegetable accompaniment with *ăn cơm* meals. On occasions, try it with **Shaking Beef (page 77)** or **Lemongrass Ribeye Steak Noodle Salad (page 97).**

Serves 2

1 tbsp vegetable oil
1 small round shallot
3 garlic cloves, finely chopped
1 chayote, peeled, sliced thinly into half moons
1 tsp butter
2 tsp oyster sauce
1 tsp maple syrup
20 g (¾ oz) herb of choice, coarsely chopped or torn
freshly ground black pepper
juice of ¼ lemon
zest of ½ lemon

Heat the vegetable oil in a wok on a high heat, add the shallots and cook until golden. Add the garlic and fry until you can smell it and it's starting to turn crisp. Immediately add the chayote and wait for 30 seconds, then stir-fry vigorously. Add the butter, oyster sauce and maple syrup and continue to fry quickly. Add the herbs, season with black pepper and toss the pan for 3 minutes, when this should be done. Serve with a good squeeze of lemon juice and lemon zest.

Note
• If you can't get hold of chayote, you can use courgette (zucchini), squash, kohlrabi, turnip or celeriac (celery root).

  SHARING VEGETABLES

FRIED COURGETTE FLOWERS WITH PRAWNS & CHIVES

HOA BÍ CHIÊN NHÂN TÔM HẸ

Here, I have combined a few things I love: Italian courgette flowers, Japanese tempura and Vietnamese herbs. Serve as a snack or over rice vermicelli (page 202).

Serves 3–4

For the prawn stuffing
165 g (5½ oz) king prawns, excess water removed and patted dry
2 garlic cloves, crushed
½ tsp caster (superfine) sugar
¼ tsp freshly ground black pepper
1 tsp fish sauce
juice of ¼ lime
finely chopped zest of ½ lime
30 g (1 oz) garlic chives, sliced into 2 cm (¾ in) pieces
60 g (2 oz) courgette (zucchini) flowers (12), centre pistil or stamens removed
400 ml (13 fl oz/generous 1½ cups) vegetable oil or enough to fill your pan 5 cm (2 in) deep

For the dressing/dipping sauce
1 bird's eye chilli, finely chopped
1 garlic clove, crushed
2 tbsp maple syrup
2 tbsp fish sauce
juice and finely chopped zest of ½ lime or lemon
10 g (¼ oz) mint leaves, finely chopped
10 g (¼ oz) coriander stems, finely sliced (2 mm)

For the courgette salad
2 courgettes (zucchini), sliced into 1 cm (½ in) rings or 12 baby courgettes, halved

For the batter
50 g (2 oz) plain (all-purpose) flour
¼ tsp baking powder
¼ tsp Japanese ichimi chilli powder (or normal)
¼ tsp ground ginger
½ tsp caster (superfine) sugar
pinch of salt
120 ml (4 fl oz/½ cup) cold sparkling water
3 ice cubes

To make the prawn stuffing, in a small blender, combine the prawns, garlic, sugar, black pepper, fish sauce, lime and lime zest. Blitz on pulse a few times so that it is still coarse but forms a paste, then marinate in the fridge for 30–60 minutes. Then let come to room temperature for about 20 minutes.

Meanwhile, mix together all the dressing ingredients. On a griddle pan, grill the courgettes until soft and charred.

Mix the garlic chives into the prawn stuffing. Stuff each courgette flower with 2 teaspoons of prawn mixture, leaving some room at the top to twist the flowers closed.

To make the batter, combine all the dry ingredients. When ready to fry, gradually add the cold sparkling water a little at a time – the amount you need will vary – and stir to combine to a smooth double cream texture, breaking up any lumps. Then add the ice cubes.

To fry the courgette flowers, heat a deep fat fryer or oil in a deep pan to 140°C (280°F) or until it fizzes with small bubbles when you put a pair of wooden chopsticks into the oil.

Cook the flowers a few at a time so you don't overcrowd the fryer basket or pan. Dip the flowers in the batter, shake off any excess, then fry on a medium–high heat for about 2–3 minutes until golden brown, or until the filling is cooked. It should fry with lots of bubbles, slowly turning golden. Rest and drain on kitchen paper. Repeat with the other flowers.

Place the courgettes and fried flowers onto a platter for everyone to share with the dipping sauce on the side.

3 PROPER SALADS, VIETNAMESE-STYLE

When I talk about salads, you can be sure there's no iceberg lettuce in sight, and I definitely don't mean the salads you're supposed to eat if you go on a diet. Vietnamese salads are what culinary dreams are made of – they are amazing!

Regarded more as treats than some kind of punishment, they are a riot of leaves, herbs, cucumber, noodles, pickles and deliciously cooked meat. I enjoy all sorts of versions of Vietnamese salads: rolled up with a fried savoury crêpe or inside a salad wrap; served with the best cut of beef or a caramelised pork belly; accompanying poached meat and sliced vegetables. These are exciting ways to enjoy leaves, making eating your greens an absolute pleasure.

Vietnamese salads are dressed with sweet and syrupy fish sauce or an acidic lime or vinegar dressing, while the zest and fiery chillies add a satisfying kick to the palate.

These salads are sometimes served over noodles or with crackers, rice paper or rice, which make these bowls a complete meal balanced with plenty of food groups and lots of exciting and exhilarating flavours. The herbs, known as perfumed leaves, excite our sense of smell as well as taste, feel and sight.

It is good to have lots of leaves and herbs for these recipes – in fact, it is frowned upon to not have enough or to display a lack of variety or an unbalanced selection. This is great as you'll probably end up eating more leaves at one sitting than you normally would in a week. They are there to lift and complement the cooked elements of the salad. These recipes are perfect to eat, especially when you can include your own homegrown herbs from the garden, balcony or window sill.

PROPER SALADS, VIETNAMESE-STYLE

SHAKING BEEF WITH WATERCRESS SALAD & TOMATO RICE

BÒ LÚC LẮC

This is very special and is a great treat to serve to visitors. My uncle, Chú Hiền, claims Maggi seasoning is his secret ingredient. This dish is usually enjoyed with tomato rice but it is also really good with Homemade Chips (page 205).

Serves 4

For the tomato rice
300 g (10½ oz) jasmine rice
500 ml (17 fl oz/2 cups) water or chicken stock
2 tbsp tomato ketchup
2 garlic cloves, whole
1 tsp mushroom seasoning (optional)

For the beef
600 g (1 lb 4 oz) grass-fed, free-range beef fillet
    or ribeye, cut into 2 cm (¾ in) cubes
1 tbsp oyster sauce
2 tbsp Maggi seasoning or soy sauce
4 garlic cloves, crushed
1 round shallot, finely chopped
1 tsp garlic powder
½ tsp caster (superfine) sugar
2 tsp sesame oil
1 heaped tsp freshly ground black pepper
2 tbsp vegetable oil, for frying

For the salad
2 tbsp cider vinegar
juice of ½ lime
1½ tbsp maple syrup or agave nectar
freshly ground black pepper
1 red onion, thinly sliced
200 g (7 oz) watercress
100 g (3½ oz) lamb's lettuce or pea shoots
200 g (7 oz) choice of tomato varieties, sliced

Start by cooking the tomato rice in either a rice cooker or saucepan. To cook in a rice cooker, wash the rice three times, then add the remaining ingredients. Cook.

To cook in a saucepan, wash the rice three times, then add the remaining ingredients. Cook the rice on a medium–low heat with the lid on. When the liquid has seeped into the rice and there isn't any water on the surface, turn the heat to low and cook with the lid securely on for a further 15–18 minutes. Turn the heat off without removing the lid and let it rest for 5–10 minutes. Fluff up the rice with a rice paddle or wooden spoon.

Combine the beef and all the ingredients in a bowl and marinate for at least 1 hour at room temperature. If you want to leave it longer, put it in the fridge, then bring to room temperature before cooking.

Meanwhile, prepare the salad dressing by shaking together the cider vinegar and lime juice with the maple syrup or agave nectar and lots of black pepper in a jar. Add the onions and leave for about 20 minutes, then pour over the salad leaves and toss together well.

You will cook the beef in batches, depending on the size of your pan. Heat a frying pan (skillet) over a high heat for a few minutes until very hot. Add 1 tablespoon of vegetable oil, then add a batch of beef cubes, making sure they are not too crowded together. Leave to sear for 30 seconds, then shake the pan vigorously for 10 seconds every 30 seconds for 1½ minutes for medium rare. Set aside on a plate to rest while you cook the remaining beef. When the beef is done, pour any juices left in the pan onto it.

Serve with the salad and tomato rice.

CHICKEN SALAD WITH SUGAR SNAP PEAS, VIETNAMESE CORIANDER & SHALLOTS

GỎI GÀ HÀNH TÍM ĐẬU HÀ LAN

This is a version of a classic salad that is seen at all celebrations, even if it is a weekend gathering. Don't let that stop you from enjoying a burst of flavour on a weeknight. You can use up a leftover roast chicken or buy a cooked rotisserie chicken. You don't have to poach the chicken from scratch if you have leftovers. But if you do poach a whole chicken you can make Chicken Phở (page 136) use half the chicken meat for that and half for a salad. Prep the vegetables beforehand and assemble when you are ready to serve.

Serves 6–8

For the salad
1.5 kg (3 lb 5 oz) whole corn-fed, free-range, organic chicken
400 g (14 oz) sugar snap peas, thinly sliced lengthways
10 radishes, thinly sliced
10 Vietnamese coriander (cilantro) sprigs, leaves picked (or Thai basil, mint or coriander), roughly snipped
small handful of coriander (cilantro), roughly chopped
handful of roughly chopped pistachios
seeds of ½ pomegranate (optional)

For the dressing
5 tbsp crushed pistachios
3 bird's eye chillies, de-seeded and finely chopped
1 garlic clove, finely chopped
3 tbsp maple syrup
5 tbsp lime juice (from about 2–3 limes)
5 tbsp fish sauce

For the shallot pickle
4 round shallots, sliced as thinly as possible
3 tbsp cider vinegar
1 tbsp caster (superfine) sugar
pinch of sea salt and freshly ground black pepper

To serve
prawn crackers

Fill a very large saucepan with 3 litres (100 fl oz/12½ cups) of boiling water, season with salt and add the chicken. Reduce to a simmer, cover and poach for 60–80 minutes (depending on the size of your chicken) until the juices run clear when you pierce the thickest part of the thigh and the chicken is cooked all the way through.

Mix the radishes, sugar snap peas and any other vegetables you're using in a large salad bowl. Add the Vietnamese coriander.

Mix together all the remaining dressing ingredients in a screw-topped jar and shake well. Taste for the balance of sweet, sour, salty and heat and adjust as necessary.

To make the shallot pickle, mix the shallots with the vinegar, sugar and a pinch of salt and pepper in a small bowl. Set aside for about 20 minutes.

When the chicken is cooked, leave to cool. Tear off the meat along the grain and season with pepper. Add this to the salad bowl along with the pickled shallots and its juices.

When ready to serve, toss the salad together with the dressing. Garnish with the coriander, pistachios and pomegranate seeds. Serve the salad with the prawn crackers or chicken broth rice.

Note

- Try swapping out the sugar snap peas for carrot, papaya, kohlrabi, daikon, courgettes (zucchini), mangetout (snow peas) or a combination of your favourites.
- You can use the chicken stock to make a delicious chicken rice.

CARAMELISED PORK BELLY SLICES & PATTIES NOODLE SALAD

BÚN CHẢ

The irresistible sweet, treacly smell of barbecued patties and caramelised pork is luring and mouth-watering. They sit on a pillow of thin rice vermicelli (*bún*) and crunchy sweet and sour pickles with plenty of refreshing herbs and leaves as salad. A large, warm, sweet and umami bowl of dipping sauce with pickles, garlic and chillies serves as a bath for the meats to soak in. You can either dip or bathe your meat in this delicious broth, or pour it over your noodles and slurp them up.

Serves 4

For the caramel sauce
60 g (2 oz) caster (superfine) sugar
75 ml (2½ fl oz) hot water

For the meat
450–500 g (1–1 lb 2 oz) free-range pork belly, skin removed, minced or blended in food processor
450–500 g (1–1 lb 2 oz) free-range pork belly, skin removed, sliced into 3 cm (1 in) squares 1 cm (⅓ in) thick
½ tbsp groundnut (peanut) or vegetable oil

For the marinade
4 garlic cloves, minced
2 round shallots, finely chopped
2 tbsp oyster sauce
1 tbsp brown sugar
4 tbsp fish sauce
1 tsp seasoning powder or stock cube (mushroom, pork or chicken) (optional)
½ tsp freshly ground black pepper

For the pickles
100 g (3½ oz) thinly sliced kohlrabi or radishes
100 g (3½ oz) thinly sliced carrots into rounds
1 tsp sea salt
1 tsp caster (superfine) sugar
2 tbsp cider vinegar

For the noodles
300 g (10½ oz) rice vermicelli (0.8 mm, page 202)

For the dipping sauce
80 ml (3 fl oz/scant ½ cup) fish sauce
100 g (3½ oz) caster (superfine) sugar
400 ml (13 fl oz/generous 1½ cups) boiling water
3 garlic cloves, finely chopped
3 chillies, finely chopped

For the garnish
fresh lettuce and herbs such as Thai basil, mint, coriander (cilantro) or perilla (shiso), etc.

To make the caramel sauce, melt the sugar in a heavy-bottomed saucepan over a low heat for about 7–10 minutes until it turns golden and caramel, swirling every now and again to move the sugar. Turn off the heat then – with extreme caution – pour the hot water into the caramel. Mix well then set aside.

Place the pork mince and sliced pork belly into two separate bowls. Mix the marinade ingredients in a bowl and divide evenly between the two bowls of meat. Then top with 2 tablespoons of the caramel sauce and mix well. Form 5-cm-wide patties with the minced pork, and place in a container. Set both aside in the fridge to marinate for at least 2 hours or overnight.

Meanwhile, prepare the pickles. Mix the carrot and kohlrabi in a bowl with the salt and rest for 15 minutes – this removes the moisture and gives it crunch. Rinse well and slightly squeeze out any remaining water. In a large bowl, mix the kohlrabi and carrots with the sugar and vinegar. Set aside for at least 1 hour in the fridge so that the veggies can absorb the flavour.

Cook the noodles as described on page 202, or according to the packet instructions.

Add a large handful of leaves to four bowls, then top each bowl with the noodles and divide half of the pickles amongst them.

Make the dipping sauce by adding all the ingredients to a bowl then giving it a good stir. Divide it among four small bowls and add the remainder of the pickles with the pickle juice.

Using a non-stick frying pan, on a medium to high heat, place the patties clockwise from 12 o'clock. Cook until golden on both sides for about 10 minutes, flipping every 2 minutes. Set aside on kitchen paper.

On a medium–high heat, in the same frying pan, add the oil and fry a batch of the pork belly (don't crowd them) until it is caramelised and golden, turning occasionally. Place the pork on kitchen paper to drain the fat. Wipe the excess oil from the pan after each batch, leaving just a touch of fat to cook the next batch.

Place half of the patties and slices of pork on each of the noodle bowls and the other half on each of the medium dipping sauce bowls.

RECIPE PICTURE IS OVERLEAF →

SIZZLING CRÊPES WITH PRAWNS

BÁNH XÈO TÔM

Bánh xèo **is a light savoury crêpe, eaten with an abundance of salad leaves and herbs. There's a knack to eating these: gather a palmful of leaves and herbs into your hand, break off some crêpe, stuff the leaves, then roll it up and dip it into the sauce. You can vary the filling.**

Makes about 6

For the nước mắm– see page 208

For the crêpe batter
100 g (3½ oz/1 cup) rice flour (Asian Rose Brand, or any non-glutinous)
1 heaped tsp ground turmeric
200 ml (7 fl oz) coconut milk
200 ml (7 fl oz) water
1 spring onion (scallion), thinly sliced
½ tsp sea salt
a pinch of caster (superfine) sugar
vegetable or coconut oil, for frying

For the filling
2 round shallots, thinly sliced
200 g (7 oz) shelled, de-veined and halved king prawns
100 g (3½ oz) beansprouts
50 g (2 oz) garlic chives or coriander (cilantro) (optional)
sea salt and freshly ground black pepper

For the garnish
lettuce leaves
spring onions (scallions), cut into short lengths
a variety of Asian herbs, such as coriander (cilantro), Thai sweet basil, garden mint, perilla (shiso), cockscomb

Notes   ◆ You can make a batch in advance. To serve, place in a very hot oven for 5 minutes to crisp up.

Wash and dry the salad leaves and set them aside.

To make the fish sauce, follow the instructions on page 208.

Next, make the crêpe batter. Mix together the flour, turmeric, coconut milk, water, spring onion, salt and sugar in a bowl, making sure it is smooth and free of lumps. It should resemble the consistency of single cream.

To make the filling, heat 1 teaspoon of oil in a frying pan (skillet) over a medium–high heat and fry a few slices of shallot until golden. Season the prawns with salt and pepper and add a couple of pieces to the pan for a minute.

Using a shallow ladle, pour in a thin layer of the crêpe batter, swivelling the pan to get it covered all around the edges. Add a handful of beansprouts and chives and cover the pan with the lid. Keep the steam in and allow to cook for 2 minutes with the lid on.

Remove the lid and cook for a further minute, making sure the crêpe is crisp and golden. Fold the crêpe in half, serve or set aside. Repeat this process with the remaining shallots, batter and other ingredients to make the rest of the crêpes.

RECIPE PICTURE IS ON PAGE 83

PAPAYA SALAD WITH PORK BELLY, PRAWNS & POMELO

GỎI ĐU ĐỦ BƯỞI TÔM THỊT

Typically at celebrations, pork belly is the prized cut that will make several appearances. It pairs particularly well with prawns and seafood and green papaya, and the perfect balance in the dressing makes this dish such a winner. Having a variety of poached or steamed seafood, such as scallops, razor clams and crab in this salad makes it even more special.

Serves 4

For the salad

300 g (10½ oz) free-range pork belly, fat and skin on
1 heaped tsp sea salt
½ green papaya, peeled and julienned
2 carrots, julienned
½ kohlrabi, julienned
1 sharp green dessert apple, such as a Granny
    Smith, cored, sliced 3 mm (⅛ in) thick and
    submerged in water with the juice of ½ lemon,
    then drained
10 stems of Vietnamese coriander (cilantro), leaves
    only, snipped into 2 cm (¾ in) pieces
175 g (6 oz) cooked, peeled king prawns
¼ pink pomelo, peeled, skin removed and flesh cut
    into 3 cm (1 in) chunks (optional)
seeds of ½ pomegranate
20 g (¾ oz) coriander (cilantro) sprigs

For the dressing

2 tbsp maple syrup
3 tbsp fish sauce
3 tbsp cider vinegar
2 garlic cloves, crushed
1 bird's eye chilli, finely chopped
3 tbsp salted, roasted peanuts,
    coarsely chopped or crushed

Pour boiling water over the pork belly and leave for 5 minutes. Drain, discard the water and rinse the pork.

Bring a small pan of water to the boil, then add the pork and a heaped teaspoon of salt, return to a simmer, cover and poach the pork for 35 minutes, or until the juices run clear. Remove from the broth (which can be kept for a soup) and cool to room temperature, then thinly slice.

Meanwhile, prepare the papaya, carrots, kohlrabi, apple and coriander, and mix together in a large mixing bowl. Add the pork and prawns and toss well together.

Shake all the dressing ingredients together and pour over the salad.

Place onto a serving plate, scatter pomelo, pomegranate and coriander over the salad and serve immediately with steamed rice (page 195) or prawn crackers.

Notes
- Buy small and pale pomegranates for lovely sweeter seeds. Green-skinned pomelo are usually pink inside.
- You can use chicken instead of pork.
- If you can't get green papaya, use more kohlrabi, carrot or white cabbage. If you can't get pomelo, just leave it out.

FRESH SALAD ROLLS

GỎI CUỐN

The ability to roll one of these is a life skill, learned from childhood. Translated as salad rolls, they are the talking point of many parties and get togethers, where guests are presented with an array of fresh leaves and herbs, accompanied with a variety of fillings: from Saigon's speciality of poached pork and prawns to baked fish. You can be as inventive or as simple as you wish.

Wash and spin or air dry the leaves, cook and slice your ingredients. Once all the ingredients are ready, make sure they are dry (to keep the paper from breaking later on). Place them on your work surface in separate containers ready to make the rolls. Pour some cold tap water into a tray deep and wide enough to hold the rice paper. Dip the paper into the tray for one second then place onto a chopping board.

Imagine if the round paper is a face (and you are standing on the left side of the opposite image). At the bottom centre of the paper, where the mouth would be, line up your main ingredients, then the herbs, noodles and lettuce. Fold the two sides in – where the ears would be – then fold up the bottom flap – the chin – to cover the ingredients. It should look like you are making an envelope. Then, as tightly as possible, starting from the bottom, roll and push down as you go along until you have reached the end of the rice paper. Keep the rolls in an airtight container at room temperature and serve within 2–3 hours, depending on the weather (or the indoor heating or air conditioning). If seafood, for example, you should serve and eat them straight away. On page 91 you will find a few of my favourite combinations and sauces.

Makes 6

For the rolls
200 g (7 oz) poached free-range pork belly, skin
   removed, thinly sliced
165 g (5½ oz) cooked prawns, shelled and de-veined
80 g (3 oz) vermicelli noodles, rehydrated
   (page 202)
12 coriander (cilantro) stems and leaves,
   roughly chopped
18 mint leaves, roughly chopped
3 sprigs cockscomb mint (optional)
18 perilla (shiso) leaves (optional)
6 garlic chives (optional)
6 lettuce leaves
6 x 22 m (9 in) rice paper sheets

For the hoisin, garlic and chilli dipping sauce
1 tsp vegetable oil
1 garlic clove, finely chopped
2 tbsp hoisin sauce
½ tbsp white wine vinegar or cider vinegar
1 tsp caster (superfine) sugar
½ tbsp chilli sauce
1 tbsp water
2 tbsp peanuts, crushed or blended

For baked salmon, avocado and beetroot
2 salmon fillets, baked with 3 tbsp teriyaki sauce
   for 12 minutes at 200°C (400°F/gas 8)
1 yellow beetroot, sliced into 1 cm (¾ in) rings,
   baked for 20 minutes at 200°C (400°F/gas 8)
1 avocado, sliced lengthways
3 dill sprigs, finely chopped
12 coriander (cilantro) stems and leaves

For the nut butter dipping sauce
1 tsp vegetable oil
1 shallot, finely chopped
1 bird's eye chilli, finely chopped
2 tbsp cashew, almond or peanut butter
2 tsp soy sauce or tamari
1 tsp maple syrup
2 tbsp water

For summer roll parties, get people making their
own rolls. Teaching everyone how to roll them
breaks the ice, it is great fun and adds to your street
cred! You can create some of these recipes, bring
them to the table with an abundance of fresh herbs
and leaves, make plenty of sauces, noodles and
supply a host of rice paper. Instant party!

For other fillings
Omelette with Carrot, Cabbage & Chinese Sausage
   (page 46)
Roast Barbecued Pork (page 101)
Crispy Roast Pork Belly (page 98)
Sea Bass Parcels with Ginger & Kimchi (page 43)
Seafood Spring Rolls (inside a fresh roll!) (page 112)
Lemongrass Ribeye Steak Noodle Salad (page 97)
Shaking Beef with Watercress Salad & Tomato
   (page 77)

To prepare the sauces, heat the oil in a saucepan
and fry the garlic or shallots until lightly browned.
Add everything else except the nuts and bring
to a gentle boil. Pour the sauce into dipping bowls
and sprinkle crushed nuts on top.

4 FEASTING

Whether you are a mediative cook or just crave these Vietnamese treats, cooking Vietnamese will satisfy your inner chef and turn you into a bit of a feeder – taking your own nourishment from other people's enjoyment of food. It is why I have always enjoyed cooking for so many people. I love the moment that people take their first bite, lose themselves in the flavours, and follow their contented quietness with a simple nod. 'Hmmm.'

For the Vietnamese, feasts are big feasts. There is never a compromise in this culture; you will always go out of your way to make a feast or not have one at all. My mum and her friends were refugees in the 1970s–80s and have always had feasts, even though their budgets have never been very big. 'Let's have a summer roll party,' someone would suggest, then they would pile up at said person's flat, each bringing an element: rice paper, lettuce or dipping sauce and so on.

On the table, there is always an oasis of rolls, dipping sauces, salads, leaves, dumplings and a noodle soup to finish off. In the corner, the old ladies loudly sing out karaoke songs, dancing together and dreaming they are pop stars in their beautiful youth. Most importantly, they feel a sense of belonging at home together even though they are continents from it.

Foods like these fashion strong memories and shape our senses – especially of the children who will then grow up to love Vietnamese food. Cooking becomes akin to escapism, a pleasure and a deep display of love rather than a chore.

As a guest at a feast, you have to keep up with the etiquette and that is to eat and enjoy what anyone gives you no matter how full you are. Serve others before you serve yourself.

LEMONGRASS RIBEYE STEAK NOODLE SALAD

BÚN BÒ XÀO

This is so vibrant, fresh and enjoyable; it's one of my favourite dishes. Add as much variety of greens and rainbow shoots and leaves as you like. Here, I love the crunch, peppery and floral flavours of all sorts of leaves mixed with the invigorating lime, its zest and fiery chillies. True to a Vietnamese-style salad, adding rice noodles to it makes this a complete meal balanced with lots of exciting and exhilarating flavours of the summer season.

Serves 2

For the beef
300–400 g (10½–14 oz) grass-fed, free-range ribeye steak, at room temperature for 2 hours (can also use rump, sirloin, bavette, onglet)
2 lemongrass stalks, finely chopped
2 garlic cloves, crushed
1 tbsp butter, at room temperature
1 tbsp soy sauce
1 tbsp oyster sauce
½ tbsp something sweet like maple syrup
1 tbsp vegetable oil
freshly ground black pepper
1 onion, halved and sliced
1 tbsp vegetable oil

For the salad
handful of anything green and leafy, like lamb's lettuce, watercress, rocket, lettuce
2 spring onions (scallions), white and green parts, sliced
1 tbsp vegetable oil
2 nests rice vermicelli (do 3 if really hungry), rehydrated (page 202)

For the salad dressing
½ bird's eye chilli, finely chopped
1 tbsp honey
1 tbsp fish sauce
finely chopped zest and juice of either ½ lime or ¼ lemon
2 tbsp hot water
sprig of mint leaves, finely chopped

1 heaped tbsp peanuts, pistachios or cashews, finely chopped
lots of freshly ground black pepper

For the instant carrot & kohlrabi pickle (optional) – see page 206

Slice the beef into 1 cm (½ in) strips. Mix together all the remaining beef ingredients except the onion and oil. Coat the beef in the marinade and leave for 20 minutes while you prepare the rest of the salad.

To prepare the salad, fry the spring onions gently in the oil for 5 minutes, then set aside.

To make the salad dressing, place all the ingredients into a bowl and mix well together or shake it up in a jar. Reserve the dressing until it is ready to be served at the table.

Add the noodles to one side of a salad bowl and smother with the spring onion oil. Mix the remaining leaves and put in the other side of the bowl.

To make the pickle, combine all the ingredients together in a bowl or use something pickled you already have in the fridge.

Heat a frying pan (skillet) over a high heat until very hot. Add half the vegetable oil and half the onions, fry off for a minute, then add half the beef with the marinade. Separate the pieces with a cooking utensil and leave without stirring for 1–2 minutes, then quickly turn them to the other side, cook for a further minute and repeat twice more. Repeat for the remaining onions and beef. Portion into a space on the noodle bowl.

Dress the salad at the table with the salad dressing. Add a sprinkling of nuts to the beef. Serve immediately.

CRISPY ROAST PORK BELLY

THỊT HEO QUAY

This is a proper treat and great to have as a centrepiece on celebratory occasions and dinner parties, so I suggest using the best free-range pork belly you can afford; it makes all the difference to the flavour and texture. Take noodles, pickles and pork onto your bowl and dress them with sauce.

I use a halogen oven for this, which does a great job of getting an even crisp and it's less smoky, but this recipe works in a regular oven too.

Serves 3–4

1 kg (2 lb 4 oz) free-range pork belly, with skin scored into 1 cm (⅔ in) squares (the bones should be separated and kept for another recipe)

For the marinade
1 tsp garlic powder
½ tbsp sea salt
½ tsp five-spice powder
½ tbsp soy sauce

For the skin
1 tbsp sea salt flakes
1 tbsp cider vinegar or lime juice

For the noodles
6–7 sheets per serving rice vermicelli
    or 80 g (3 oz) rice vermicelli (0.8 mm, page 202)
Spring Onion Oil (page 206)

For the sauces
Sweet Chilli and Garlic Dipping Sauce (page 208)
Instant Carrot & Kohlrabi Pickle (page 206) or pickles of choice

Place the pork in a container, skin-side up and pour boiling water from a kettle over it until submerged, then set aside for 5 minutes. Drain, then repeat once or twice. This removes excess fat (and impurities) to make sure the skin goes crisp. Drain and dab the skin dry with paper towels.

Mix the pork marinade ingredients together in a bowl. Turn the meat over and rub the marinade on the meat side. Turn the belly over to the skin side and continue to pat dry. Sprinkle with sea salt and rub in the cider vinegar. Set aside for at least 2 hours, removing any excess moisture on the skin with paper towels every 30 minutes.

Preheat the oven to 220°C (425°F/gas 8). Line a roasting tin with parchment paper and place a metal rack on top. Place the pork belly on the rack and roast for 1 hour skin-side up, then turn over for 10 minutes until the pork is tender. Leave the pork belly to cool completely.

Ideally, use a cleaver to slice up the pork. I usually turn the crispy side over by first slicing the meat and then putting pressure on the cleaver to cut the skin. You'll hear a delicious crunch. Pile the pork onto a serving dish neatly, crispy-side up.

If using a selection of leaves and herbs to make a salad, wash and display it on a plate/basket.

Cook the noodles as described on page 202, or according to the packet instructions.

Serve at room temperature with the sauces – but, if you can't wait, warm is fantastic.

Notes
• If you can't get vermicelli sheet noodles (*bánh hỏi*), use rice vermicelli or rice.

Make ahead
Marinate: 2 days
Cook: Same day, morning

ROAST BARBECUED PORK

XÁ XÍU

This is a very easy recipe that recruits most of your storecupboard ingredients to create something to intrigue your palate. *Xá xíu* is based on the Chinese *char sui*, a treat for the weekend. This can be enjoyed stuffed in a crunchy and herby *bánh mì,* homed in a steamed bao bun with extra sauce to drizzle, used as a sidekick to a Wonton Noodle Soup (page 146) and – my favourite way – on steamed rice with plenty of steamed greens and vegetables. This marinade is also great on chicken wings, thighs or pork ribs.

Serves 4

450 g (1 lb) free-range pork tenderloin or shoulder

For the marinade
50 g (2 oz) caster (superfine) sugar
2 tsp sea salt
1 tsp five-spice powder
½ tsp white pepper
1 tsp sesame oil
2 tbsp Shaoxing rice wine
1 tbsp soy sauce
1 tbsp oyster sauce
1 tbsp English mustard
1 tbsp hoisin sauce
2 tsp tomato ketchup
1 tsp garlic powder
a few drops of red food colouring (optional)

For the glaze
2 tbsp honey, coconut syrup, maple syrup
   or agave nectar
1 tsp grated ginger root
1 tbsp hot water

If you're using tenderloin, place it in a lidded glass container. If using another cut, slice the pork into long strips or chunks about 7.5 cm (3 in) thick, then place in a container.

Combine all the marinade ingredients together in a bowl. Reserve about 2 tablespoons of marinade and set it aside.

Rub the pork with the rest of the marinade. For best results, cover and refrigerate overnight, or for at least 8 hours. Cover and store the reserved marinade in the fridge. If you can't wait, just go ahead and carry on – it will still be tasty.

Preheat the oven to 250°C (400°F/gas 8). Line a roasting tin with parchment paper and place a metal rack on top. Place the pork on the rack, pour a mug of boiling water into the pan below the rack. This prevents any bits burning at the bottom but also creates a nice steam. Roast for 25 minutes.

Meanwhile, mix the 2 tablespoons of reserved marinade with the honey, ginger and 1 tablespoon of hot water.

After 25 minutes, turn the pork over and roast for another 15 minutes. Using a pastry brush, baste with the glaze and roast for another 10 minutes. Brush the glaze over again and roast for 5 more minutes. Don't walk away or it will burn.

Take it out of the oven, glaze all over and leave to rest for at least 10 minutes before serving.

This is great served hot or cold.

‿‿‿‿‿‿‿‿‿‿‿‿‿‿‿‿‿‿‿‿‿‿

Notes
- If you don't have five-spice powder, finely grind 2 star anise.
- If you don't have oyster sauce, add more soy sauce. If you don't have Shaoxing, add rice wine vinegar, sherry vinegar or cider vinegar.

Make ahead
Marinate: 2 days
Cook: 2 days

BANH BAO WITH MUSHROOMS & CHINESE SAUSAGE

BÁNH BAO NẤM LẠP XƯỞNG

These sweet, fluffy, light and milky buns are best eaten as soon as they are steamed. Fill with Roast Barbecued Pork (page 101). You'll need a two-tier bamboo steamer with the lid wrapped securely with a tea towel for this recipe.

Makes 8

For the bao filling
1 tsp vegetable oil
1 Asian or small round shallot, finely chopped
1 Chinese sausage (*lạp xưởng*), thinly sliced
140 g (5 oz) oyster mushrooms, finely chopped
60 g (2 oz) kale, hard stalks removed and leaves finely chopped
1½ tbsp soy sauce
1½ tsp caster (superfine) sugar
1 tsp sesame oil
25 g (¾ oz) glass noodles, soaked in cold water for 10 minutes, then trimmed into 3 cm (1¼ in) pieces
½ tsp freshly ground black pepper
8 quail eggs, hard-boiled and peeled

For the bao dough
250 g (9 oz/2 cups) plain (all-purpose) flour
4 g (⅛ oz) active yeast
3 g (⅛ oz) baking powder
65 ml (2 fl oz/¼ cup) water (plus extra as needed)
70 ml (2½ fl oz/¼ cup) whole milk
2 tbsp caster (superfine) sugar
½ tbsp sea salt

Warm 1 teaspoon of vegetable oil in a frying pan (skillet) over a medium heat and fry off the shallot for 3–5 minutes until lightly golden. Next add the Chinese sausage and fry for a further 3 minutes, then add the mushrooms and finally add the kale, soy sauce, sugar, black pepper and sesame oil. When everything is combined and wilted, transfer to a bowl and leave to cool. Squeeze out the juices and mix them with the glass noodles.

To make the dough, pour the flour into a large mixing bowl, add the yeast, baking powder, sugar and salt. Mix together and make a well in the centre.

Depending on the brand of the flour, the amount of water you need will vary. Pour the water into the well and slowly combine with your hands, then add the milk and bring together to form a dough. Knead together with the base of your palm, pushing forward and rolling. If the dough is stiff, add a teaspoon of water at a time. Keep kneading for about 5–10 minutes until the dough is smooth and cleanly formed and there are no crumbs or flour left on the surface.

Roll out the dough into a sausage shape about 30 cm (12 in) long, and divide into 8 pieces, each weighing approx. 50 g (2 oz). Rest inside an oiled, airtight container while you work.

Lightly dust the rolling pin with flour, roll one of the dough balls thinner on the outer rim and less so in the middle into 15 cm (6 in) circles. Take the circle into the palm of your hand, place a tablespoon of mushroom mixture in the centre and top with a quail egg.

Holding one side of rim with your thumb, use your index finger to pinch together 1 cm (½ in) of dough and gather about 16 pleats towards the thumb to close the bun. Then pinch, twist and seal the dough together. Place on a parchment square. Rest on a two-tier bamboo steamer, then repeat with the rest of the dough, making sure there is a two-finger space between them.

Place inside a cold oven with a mugful of boiling water in the bottom and rest for 50 minutes or until doubled in size. Tap the dough: if it bounces back, it's ready to be steamed.

Bring a steamer pot or low-filled pan of water to the boil. Place one of the tiers over the steamer. Cover and steam for 8–10 minutes. When the baos are cooked, leave the lid ajar for 2–3 minutes before you take them out.

BROKEN RICE WITH LEMONGRASS PORK STEAKS & STEAMED EGG PUDDING

CƠM TẤM SƯỜN

Rice is hardly ever eaten from a plate – except here; this serves as a compact lunch for busy workers. *Cơm tấm* translates as 'broken rice', a dish of inferior grains once eaten only by poor rice farmers, which has subsequently become one of the most popular dishes in Saigon. Vibrant, colourful and truly a happy meal, reflective of the way Saigonese people are – always beaming with sweet, sunny glee.

You will need a steamer for this recipe. If you can't get broken rice, use jasmine – washed and soaked for 1 hour, then crushed with your hands to break the rice.

Serves 4

For the pork shoulder & marinade
4 free-range pork shoulder steaks (about 500 g/
    1 lb 2 oz)
4 lemongrass stalks, finely chopped
2 bird's eye chillies, finely chopped
2 garlic cloves, crushed
3 tbsp coconut sugar, agave nectar, maple syrup
    or caster (superfine) sugar
4 tbsp fish sauce
1 lime juice or lemon juice plus zest, finely chopped

For the rice
300 g (10½ oz/1½ cups) broken rice

For the steamed egg pudding
85 g (2½ oz) oyster mushrooms, cut into 1 cm
    (½ in) cubes
3 eggs
2 tsp fish sauce
25 g or ½ pack of glass noodles, soaked
    for 10 minutes in cold water then cut
    into 2.5-cm (1-in) strands
1 round shallot, finely chopped
¾ tsp caster (superfine) sugar
pinch of freshly ground black pepper
2 egg yolks, beaten

To serve
Instant Carrot & Kohlrabi Pickle (page 206)
Sweet Chilli & Garlic Dipping Sauce (page 208)
Spring Onion Oil (page 206)

For the garnish
½ cucumber, thinly sliced into circles
small handful of coriander (cilantro) leaves
2 summer tomatoes, cut into bite-sized pieces
    (optional)
4 fried eggs (optional)

Mix the marinade ingredients together well and coat the pork. Refrigerate for an hour or overnight. When ready to use, bring to room temperature.

Cook the broken rice in a rice cooker or saucepan according to the instructions on page 195.

To make the pudding, fry the mushrooms with the fish sauce until wilted. Discard the liquid residue. Transfer to a small mixing bowl and beat in the eggs, noodles and seasoning.

Pour the mixture into a small heatproof dish that fits inside a steamer and steam with the lid on for 12–15 minutes. Then add the beaten egg yolk on top and steam for a further 5 minutes without the lid to retain the colour of the yolk. Set aside.

Set a large frying pan (skillet) on a high heat and sear the pork steaks on both sides for 2 minutes. Turn the heat down to low, then cook for about 6–8 minutes on each side.

Serve each portion of pork chop on a plate with broken rice, a slice of steamed egg pudding, pickles, vegetables and the dressing in individual sauce dishes. Traditionally, this is served with a fried egg, but that's entirely up to you.

ROAST POUSSIN WITH LEMON, ORANGE & GARLIC WITH ROASTED CHIPS

GÀ NƯỚNG CHANH CAM TỎI KHOAI TÂY

I love eating a good roast but if I am making one, I try to make my Sundays as fragrant as possible using ingredients I would commonly find in my kitchen: orange juice, oranges, lemons, ginger and lemongrass. Having a small supply of lime leaves in the freezer is great to add a little va-va-voom to anything. As ovens are not that common in Vietnamese homes, roast chicken is among the many eating-out favourites.

Serves 2 hungry people or 4 with loads
of vegetable sides

250 ml (9 fl oz/1 cup) freshly squeezed orange juice
2 tsp coconut syrup or maple syrup
1 tbsp fish sauce
2 x 500 g (1 lb 2 oz) poussins (Cornish hens)
2 lemongrass stalks, bashed with a rolling pin
3 lime leaves, whole (optional)
½ garlic bulb, peeled and flattened with a knife
40 g (1½ oz) ginger root, sliced
1 tbsp vegetable oil
1½ tsp sea salt
1 tsp freshly ground black pepper
½ garlic bulb, unpeeled, left whole, sliced in half
2 red onions, unpeeled, quartered
1 lemon, zested and sliced into rings
1 orange, zested and sliced into rings
4 star anise
1 tsp cornflour (cornstarch), mixed with 2 tbsp
    water, until lumps disappear

For the garnish
2 bird's eye chillies, sliced (can substitute for
    another less spicy pepper if you don't like things
    too hot) (optional)
1 spring onion (scallion), chopped

Preheat the oven to 190°C (375°F/gas 7).

In a small bowl, mix together the orange juice, coconut or maple syrup and fish sauce. Set aside.

In a roasting tin big enough for the poussins, place the bashed lemongrass, lime leaves (if using), the flattened garlic cloves and ginger slices.

Spatchcock the poussins by placing them one at a time breast-side down on a chopping board, with the legs towards you. Using a good pair of kitchen scissors, cut up along each side of the backbone to remove it. Open the poussin out and turn over. With the heel of your hand, flatten the bird and spread out onto a high-sided baking tray that fits both birds snugly. Repeat with the other poussin. Save the backbone to make stock or add it to the roast for extra gravy flavour.

Rub the poussins with vegetable oil and salt around all the grooves of the birds, along the insides of the thighs and wings. Wash your hands, then season the birds with black pepper. Place them on top of the lemongrass, garlic and ginger on the tray.

Around the tray scatter the whole halved garlic bulb, onions, lemon and orange pieces. Pour over the sauce mixture, rubbing it into the skin of the poussin, then place the star anise on the poussin. Roast the poussin for 45–55 minutes or more until the juices run clear when the thickest part is pierced with a skewer, basting every 15 minutes.

Rest the poussins for 10 minutes, then pour the juices into a small saucepan and bring to the boil. Add the cornflour mixture and whisk it in to avoid any lumps in the gravy, stirring well to thicken.

Garnish with chillies, if you like, the citrus zest and spring onion. Serve with Homemade Chips (page 205) or steamed rice (page 195) and plenty of vegetable sides.

FRIED CHICKEN WINGS

GÀ CHIÊN KIỂU VIỆT NAM

Fried chicken has an ability to bring people together through the shameless grabbing and gnawing. The only audacity is to eat it with a knife and fork. As it is a guilty pleasure, I've made it extra sweet and extra sour, and you can make it extra spicy if you wish. If you want to make ahead and double fry: fry them in batches, then re-fry for another 2 minutes just before serving. Make loads, invite the neighbours, enjoy the pleasure.

Serves 2

For deep-frying
400 ml (13 fl oz/generous 1½ cups) vegetable oil
   or enough to fill your pan 5 cm (2 in) deep

For the marinade
400–500 g (14–1 lb 2 oz) chicken wings, jointed
1½ tsp garlic powder
1 tbsp fish sauce
½ tsp black pepper
½ tbsp cider vinegar
½ tbsp brown sugar

For the batter
60 g (2 oz) potato starch or cornflour (cornstarch)
¼ tsp ground ginger
¼ tsp cayenne pepper
¼ tsp sea salt
½ tsp caster (superfine) sugar
½ tsp baking powder
½ tsp freshly ground black pepper

For the sauce
2–3 bird's eye chillies with seeds,
   finely chopped
2 garlic cloves, finely chopped
zest of 1 lime, finely chopped
1½ tbsp lime juice
2 tbsp marmalade
2 tbsp caster (superfine) sugar
2 tbsp fish sauce
1 tbsp chopped coriander stalks or sliced spring
   onion (scallion) (optional)
1 tsp sesame oil

For the garnish
spring onion (scallion), finely chopped
chillies, de-seeded and finely chopped
an array of lettuce and herbs of choice to wrap
   the chicken meat (optional)
Sweet Chilli & Garlic Dipping Sauce (page 208)

Mix the marinade ingredients together in a small bowl and coat the chicken wings. Marinate for at least 30 minutes at room temperature or in the fridge overnight.

Mix the sauce ingredients together and set aside.

Prepare any garnishes and salad baskets.

Whisk the batter ingredients in another bowl.

Heat a deep-fat fryer to 160°C (320°F) or heat oil in a pan. To check that it is hot enough, dip a pair of wooden chopsticks into the oil and it should fizz about 1 cm (½ in) bubbles. Heat the oven to 120°C (250°F) to keep the wings warm.

Coat one batch of wings in the batter mix, going into all the nooks and crannies, then leave to rest on a plate for 5 minutes. Shake off any excess batter mix and gently place a few into the pan of oil, without overcrowding, and deep-fry for 5–6 minutes until golden and the juices run clear, then remove from the oil and drain on paper towels. Transfer them to the oven to keep warm and crisp. Reheat the oil and keep adding batches until you have cooked all the wings.

To serve, pour the sauce all over the chicken wings, garnish with spring onion and chillies and serve with the dipping sauce. This can be served with noodles, rice, salad wraps or simply enjoyed as is.

ENGLISH NIGHT FISH & CHIPS

CÁ VÀ KHOAI TÂY CHIÊN KIỂU ANH

Make your own breadcrumbs easily from any leftover bread. I really like Turkish bread; it fries really well and has a great flavour, and if you make it into breadcrumbs, you can keep it in a jar for many uses. Use Asian ingredients to vamp it up a notch, or feel free to leave out the chillies if you are serving kids. This is a household favourite, though it is not strictly Vietnamese. We used to have English nights when we were little with fish fingers and we loved it. Sometimes you need something plainer, simple and delicious too.

Serves 4

For the fish
8–10 heaped tbsp Homemade Breadcrumbs
    (page 205)
4 tbsp plain (all-purpose) flour
2 eggs
2 spring onions (scallions), sliced
½ bunch of coriander (cilantro) stalks,
    cut into 5 mm (¼ in) pieces
sea salt and freshly ground black pepper
4 lemon sole, sea bass or sea bream fillets
4 tbsp vegetable oil, for frying
4 lime leaves (optional)

To serve
Homemade Chips (page 205)
Sweet Chilli & Mango Sauce (page 209)
1 lemon, cut into 4 wedges

Place four large dinner plates on the work surface, adding flour to the first one, egg to the second and breadcrumbs, sliced spring onion, sliced coriander stalks and a good pinch of salt and pepper to the third plate.

Wash and pat dry the fish fillets, then dust a piece in flour until it is evenly coated, then dip it into the egg plate to coat on each side. Finally place the fish onto the breadcrumb and spring onion plate so that the fish takes up the crumbs, then turn to cover the other side. Then place onto the empty fourth plate. Repeat this process for the other fillets.

Heat 1 tablespoon of oil per fish in a frying pan (skillet) over a medium–high heat. Add the fish and a lime leaf, if using, per fish in batches so the pan is not overcrowded, and shallow-fry, skin-side down first, for 4 minutes on each side.

Serve with chips, mango sauce and lemon wedges.

SEAFOOD SPRING ROLLS

CHẢ GIÒ HẢI SẢN

When we were little, my mum won many new friends when she brought a platter of her spring rolls to school or served them at our birthday parties. You can use Chinese wrapper paper but I adore the crisp and blisters you get with rice paper. These are a real treat when they are homemade and are loved by everyone. When frying in batches, keep the cooked rolls hot and crispy in the oven, or freeze the rolls and deep-fry from frozen.

Makes 12

165 g (5½ oz) raw king prawns, shelled, de-veined, patted dry and coarsely chopped
150 g (5 oz) tinned, frozen or fresh crab meat, moisture pressed out
80 g (3 oz) scallops, patted dry and roughly chopped (optional)
125 g (4 oz) parsnips, julienned
120 g (4 oz) carrots, julienned
75 g (2½ oz) beansprouts
25 g (¾ oz) glass noodles, soaked in cold water for 10 minutes, drained and trimmed to 3 cm (1 in)
½ tbsp maple syrup
½ tsp mushroom or chicken seasoning
pinch of coarsely ground black pepper
2 pinches of sea salt
2 spring onions (scallions), thinly sliced
2 garlic cloves, finely chopped
12 sheets spring roll rice paper, about 22 cm (8.5 in)
1 litre (34 fl oz/4 cups) sunflower or vegetable oil

For the garnish
1 lettuce, leaves separated
an array of herbs of choice: coriander (cilantro), Vietnamese coriander (cilantro), mint, perilla (shiso)
Nước mắm (page 208)

Prepare all the spring roll filling ingredients and combine well together in a large bowl.

Put a pan or wok of oil on a medium-high heat until it reaches about 160°C (320°F). If you don't have a thermometer, the oil is ready if you dip a pair of wooden chopsticks in and it sizzles and bubbles.

Prepare a tray of warm water and dip a piece of rice paper in it to moisten for 1 second, then place it on a clean chopping board. Spoon 2 tablespoons of filling into the bottom middle – where the mouth would be if it were a face. Wait a minute for the paper to soften. Fold in the two sides, as if you are making an envelope, then fold up the bottom flap. Using your fingers to secure the roll, push forward and tuck in as you roll towards the top of the paper making sure it is tight. Repeat until you have made all the rolls. Deep-fry at 160°C (320°F/gas 4), for 4–5 minutes, or until golden brown, with space between the rolls so that they do not stick together. Serve immediately with lettuce, herbs (wrapped around the spring roll), dipping sauce and/or with a vermicelli noodle salad.

Make ahead

Make: Way ahead – can deep-fry from frozen
Filling: 1 day (but don't leave them wrapped in the paper as they will get soggy all day)
Sauce: 2 days

BÁNH MÌ

BÁNH MÌ

It is quite hard to get a decent Vietnamese baguette, so if you want to make a perfect filled *bánh mì* you'll need to make your own. Of course, French baguettes will do if you cannot. Vietnamese baguettes are light and fluffy on the inside and crispy on the outside. The crust is golden but thin; it makes an irresistible crackling noise when it is held and then bitten. They are filled with different textures and flavours of meat, herbs, vegetables, spice and seasoning. It is the perfect sandwich in taste, in size and lightness.

Please note that it takes time to make these and that it is best to just follow the recipe as precisely as you can to achieve the best results. As well as your usual baking equipment, a water sprayer and a baguette tray are useful for this recipe. If you don't have a baguette tray, you can make do with an oven baking rack, three tins of unopened canned food, a piece of baking parchment that fits the rack and some scissors or a hole puncher.

Makes 6 baguettes

PART ONE:
STARTER

Make the starter in the evening so it is for the morning. It will take about 8–10 hours to complete the process.

For the starter
150 g (5 oz) strong white (bread) flour or anything
    with 11–13 per cent protein content
½ tsp sea salt
2 g instant yeast
90 ml (3 fl oz/⅓ cup) cold water

Mix together the ingredients, then knead for about 2 minutes. Seal in an airtight container or bag for 8–10 hours at room temperature or 24 hours in the fridge. If it has been in a fridge, leave at room temperature for at least an hour before you want to use it.

PART TWO:
COMBINE THE INGREDIENTS

For the baguette
300 g (10½ oz/scant 3 cups) strong white (bread)
    flour, plus extra for dusting
½ tsp instant yeast
1 heaped tsp sea salt
1 tbsp vegetable oil
1 egg, plus cold water to make up 190 g (7 fl oz/
    scant 1 cup) in total, mixed

Place the starter and all the bread ingredients in the bowl of a mixer, fit the dough hook and knead on the lowest setting for 15 minutes. If you don't have a mixer, knead by hand and combine until you get a very smooth and elastic dough. It should still be wet and sticky, so try to only use a little flour for dusting.

Oil the bowl lightly, lay the dough inside, cover and place into a cold oven with 300 ml (10 fl oz/ ¼ cups) of boiling water for 1 hour 15 minutes.

PART THREE:
SHAPING

If you don't have a baguette tray, place a clean dish towel on a baking tray, and lightly dust it with flour. Make a space for each baguette by marking three rows of two 2.5-cm (1-in) wide spaces on the towel, with at least 5 cm (2 in) between each baguette. You can hold the towel in place with a few tins at the bottom to stop it from moving.

After 75 minutes, the dough should have risen and at least doubled in size. Lightly dust a clean surface and push the dough out into a square shape with your hands. Fold in all the corners until you have a ball and keep shaping the dough into a round ball. Lay the folds at the bottom. Repeat twice.

As fast as you can, divide the dough into two and then each piece into three, making six balls. Take each ball and stretch it out into a square, folding in the corners, then shape into a ball. Rest on the dish towel tray for 5 minutes.

After 5 minutes, repeat the previous process and rest again for 5 minutes.

Lightly dust the rolling pin, roll out a dough into a pear shape, small at the top and fat at the bottom then roll from the top down firmly with three fingers from each hand. Then continue to roll the dough into a long baguette shape, with more force on the ring and little finger to make pointy ends. Place onto the dish-towel tray.

Repeat with the other pieces of dough. Cover the shaped doughs with a dish towel. Place in the switched-off oven with two mugs filled with boiling water to prove for 60 minutes until doubled in size.

Get the next stage ready while you wait. You can also make fillings and prep the herbs and vegetables.

PART FOUR:
BAKING

If you don't have a baguette tray, take a baking rack that fits the oven, measure out the same size baking parchment, fold it into 2.5 cm (1 in) folds and cut tiny triangle shapes along the paper on both edges, 2.5 cm (1 in) apart. If you have a hole puncher, this will be easier and quicker. This is so that the steam can distribute evenly later on.

Remove the dough and mugs from the oven and preheat to 260°C (500°F/gas 10).

Carefully place the dough on the baguette tray or rack. They will feel irresistibly soft and pillowy, like clouds.

Spray evenly with water. With a sharp knife or bread slashing tool, slit the baguette lengthways at a 45 degree angle, 5 mm (½ in) deep all the way. Turn the oven temperature down to 230°C (450°F/gas 8). Fill the bottom tray with 200 ml (7 fl oz/scant 1 cup) of boiling water and place at the bottom of the oven. Bake the baguettes immediately, setting the timer for 18 minutes, spraying with water every 5 minutes. After 18 minutes, take the golden baguettes out to cool. Split in half lengthways and fill them up with all your favourite fillings.

HOW TO ASSEMBLE BÁNH MÌ

BÁNH MÌ

Bánh mì is such a favourite among the Vietnamese and all those who have ever tried it. A typical filling contains the most delightful combination of ingredients, the perfect equilibrium of sweet, umami, sour and refreshing pickles with cooling crunch, invigorating herbs and spicy heat. It is all housed in a baguette, light and fluffy inside, crispy and crunchy on the outside.

There is nothing better than eating this, with the sublime balance of flavour and textures. There are many ways to fill a *bánh mì*; here is a list of typical suggestions, but recipes can be found throughout the book to add into your roll of heaven.

Serves 1

30 cm (12 in) long Vietnamese baguette or freshly baked French baguette per serving

Spread the inside with one of these
pork or chicken liver pâté
cheese spread
butter

Use one of these cooked fillings
Fried egg
Egg & Asparagus (page 121)
Roasted Vegetables (page 121)
Roast Barbecued Pork (page 101)
Crispy Roast Pork Belly (page 98)
Fish Cakes (page 143)
Lemongrass Ribeye Steak Noodle Salad (page 97)

Or use cold cuts
Vietnamese ham (*chà lụa*), thinly sliced
Sour pickled ham (*chà nem*), thinly sliced
ham, ox tongue, roast chicken, leftovers
    or cold cuts, thinly sliced

Add some or all of these garnishes
coriander (cilantro)
mint
Thai basil or coriander (cilantro)
cucumber, cut into 10 cm (4 in) lengths,
spring onions (scallions), thinly sliced lengthways
Maggi liquid seasoning
red chillies, sliced
chilli sauce
watercress
pea shoots
summer leaves
Instant Carrot & Kohlrabi Pickle (page 206)

To assemble, split the baguette lengthways and pull out the filling. (This could be used to make breadcrumbs, page 205.) Spread with butter or similar spread. Layer with a cooked filling or cold cuts, add some garnishes of your choice – most commonly coriander, spring onion and cucumber – add some pickle, disperse chilies everywhere and squirt over a few drops of Maggi seasoning. Close the sandwich.

To pack, wrap with baking parchment and tie with a string, or place in a small airtight container.

ROASTED VEGETABLE BAGUETTE FILLING

BÁNH MÌ RAU CỦ NƯỚNG

These roasted vegetables are a great addition to a *bánh mì* but can also be used with other recipes.

Serves 4

4 x aubergines (eggplants), sliced into 1 cm
   (½ in) rings
½ courgette (zucchini), sliced into 1 cm (½ in) rings
½ fennel bulb, sliced into 1 cm (½ in) rings
1 tbsp vegetable oil or olive oil

For the shallot
½ shallot, sliced
juice of ½ lime
2 tsp clear honey
2 tsp fish sauce or soy sauce for a vegan version
juice and zest of ¼ lime, sliced into tiny cubes
1 tsp toasted sesame seeds
2.5 cm (1 in) coriander (cilantro) stalks, finely
   chopped
2.5 cm (1 in) fennel tops (optional)
½ red chilli, finely chopped (optional)

Preheat oven to 180°C (350°F/gas 6). Place the vegetables in a roasting tin and brush with a little oil, using a pastry brush, sprinkle with salt and pepper and roast for 25 minutes. You can roast any vegetables you like and can even use leftover grilled or roasted vegetables. Leave to cool for 20 minutes.

Gently brown the shallot over a medium heat. Combine the lime juice, honey and fish sauce, pour over the vegetables and cook for about 5 minutes until it has slightly reduced and thickened. Let cool for about 10 minutes. Add the lime zest, toasted sesame seeds, coriander stalks, fennel tops and chillies, if using. Pour over the vegetables and toss together.

EGG & ASPARAGUS BAGUETTE FILLING

BÁNH MÌ TRỨNG VÀ MĂNG TÂY

Serves 4

2 eggs, beaten
2 spring onions (scallions), sliced
pinch of freshly ground black pepper
½ tsp caster (superfine) sugar
pinch of sea salt
1 tsp soy sauce
1 tbsp vegetable oil
2 round shallots (40 g/1½ oz), finely chopped
4 asparagus stems, sliced diagonally 1 cm
   (½ in) thick

Beat the eggs with the spring onions, salt and pepper, sugar and soy sauce. Heat the oil in a frying pan (skillet) over a medium heat and brown off the shallots, then cook the asparagus for a minute and pour over the egg mixture to make the omelette, turning once when one side is brown. This should take no longer than a few minutes. Remove from the heat and cut into long strips.

5   HEAVENLY NOODLE SOUPS

I love a good comforting, warm and soothing noodle soup, it's my favourite and I can eat it on a daily basis no matter what the weather or season.

Light, fragrant and invigorating, noodle soups are quintessentially a breakfast dish, which is cooked the day before. What a joy to wake up to the smell of star anise and cinnamon in a steaming hot bowl of phở.

Broths are infusions; the ingredients merge and marry harmoniously. Making broth is a simple skill which anyone can easily master; some are really quick and easy to make but some take patience. Some traditional broths demand commitment and dedication for those who are really keen, but if you love broths as much as I do, you will enjoy the time it takes to nurture the broth and perfect all the toppings.

You may only want to start with the quicker recipes but whichever you choose, it is good to make as much as you can. You can freeze, refrigerate or give away what you don't need that day, then have it ready for another time. If another recipe calls for you to de-bone chicken thighs, save the bones for a quick noodle soup or freeze them for when you next cook broth.

To create a clear and flavourful broth, I always suggest that you submerge and blanch any meat and bones in hot water, simmer red meat for about 5–10 minutes, then drain, discard the water and clean before you start cooking the broth; it is standard practice.

Noodles play an important role in all of this, too. Take care of them, make sure they are not overcooked and, where possible, try to use the right sized and shaped noodles with the right broth; it does make all the difference to the finished bowl. There are certain traditional soups like *phở* and *bún bò Huế* that should not be messed with; by which I mean, try not to divert too far from these recipes.

BEEF PHỞ

PHỞ BÒ

When you fall in love with *phở* it flows through your veins and fuels your emotional well-being. I can eat this every day and never tire of it. To make *phở* takes a certain amount of love and time. The smell will fill the house with a delicious sense of home. Choose the best quality free-range, grass-fed meat and bones. Every pot of *phở* you make will taste different from the last.

Serves 8

For the stock & meat
4 litres (140 fl oz/6 cups) water
2 free-range medium oxtail, cut into 2.5 cm (1 in) chunks
1 kg (2 lb 4 oz) grass-fed, free-range beef bones/marrow
1.5 kg (2 lb 4 oz) grass-fed, free-range beef short rib
15 g (½ oz) sea salt
2 litres (3½ pints/8½ cups) homemade or good-quality chicken stock
1 large onion, cut both ends to stand
150 g (5 oz) ginger root, halved
10 cm (4 in) daikon
1 large parsnip
20 star anise
2 cinnamon sticks
6 whole cloves in a ball strainer or small muslin infuser
1 tsp coriander seeds in a ball strainer or small muslin infuser
2 black cardamom pods
50 g (2 oz/¼ cup) rock sugar
1 tbsp mushroom or chicken powder
4–5 tbsp fish sauce

For the garnish in the noodle bowl
1 red onion, thinly sliced into half rings
60 g (2 oz) coriander (cilantro), with stalks, coarsely chopped
2 spring onions (scallions), sliced lengthways, soaked in cold water until curled

For the noodles
75 g (2½ oz) per serving dry flat rice noodles or fresh wide and flat rice noodles
freshly ground black pepper

For the rare beef
70 g (2½ oz) per bowl of grass-fed, free-range beef rump steak or tips, thinly sliced (optional)

For the garnish on the table
handful of coriander (cilantro) leaves
handful of Thai basil, left on the stalks for freshness (optional)
4 bird's eye chillies, sliced diagonally
2 limes, sliced into wedges
handful of beansprouts, raw or blanched (optional)

For the table condiments
fish sauce
hoisin sauce
chilli sauce
chilli oil

To achieve a clear broth, bring a large saucepan of water to the boil, add the meat and bones and boil for 10 minutes. Remove from the heat and discard all the water. Wash the meat with tap water to remove any scum. Wash the pot clean. Fill the same pot with the fresh water and bring to the boil. Add the prepared meat, return to the boil, then add the salt, cover and simmer for 90 minutes, occasionally clearing any excess scum or fat. Then add the chicken stock. Meanwhile, place a griddle pan on a high heat and char the onion, ginger, daikon and parsnip on both sides. Add to the broth, cover and simmer for another 30 minutes. Using the same pan, lightly toast the star anise, cinnamon sticks, cloves, coriander seeds and black cardamom pods for 3–5 minutes to bring out their beautiful fragrance and flavour.

Add the toasted spices to the pot with the rock sugar and mushroom seasoning. Simmer for a further 30 minutes, keeping the lid on and skimming off any impurities every now and then.

After 2½ hours of simmering, lift out the rib meat and oxtail (leaving the bones) into a bowl of cold water for 10 minutes, then drain and put aside to rest. Leave the broth to simmer for another 30 minutes.

When the meat has cooled, slice it thinly, cover and set aside. With a long-handled spider or slotted spoon, remove all the spices, vegetables and bones from the broth. With the broth still on a simmer, season it with fish sauce, tasting for the correct amount as this could vary every time. You may need to add more mushroom seasoning or rock sugar to obtain the best flavour.

While the broth is cooking, you can prepare the garnish of red onion, coriander and spring onion, then the additional plate of herbs, chillies, lime and beansprouts for the table. Cook the noodles as described on page 202, or according to the packet instructions. To assemble, place a portion of noodles into big noodle soup bowls with a pinch of black pepper. Top with the sliced cooked meat with a generous sprinkling of coriander, spring onions and red onion, then put the thin raw slices of steak on top. To serve, pour piping hot ladles of broth over the noodles and raw rump; this should cook the steak perfectly. Everything must be submerged in the broth. Serve immediately with lime wedges and chillies, a dish of garnishes on the side and any additional condiments.

RECIPE PICTURE IS OVERLEAF →

Note
• The broth can make up to eight bowls. If you don't have guests, you can freeze the stock in portions or prepare enough ingredients for the coming days, like extra noodles and chopped herbs readily assembled in vessels so you can quickly eat a bowl by heating it all up for a snack, lunch or supper.

Make ahead
Broth: 5 days
Herbs & noodles: 2–3 days

LEMONGRASS BEEF NOODLE SOUP

BÚN BÒ HUẾ

This is a real labour of love – commit to it without shortcuts. My grandmother was from Huế, where she used to make this every morning at her home restaurant; this was what made my blood, bones and being. Having every last drop of the broth means to be home and to be loved. The garnish plate can be as elaborate or as minimal as you wish. Great additions are banana blossom, morning glory stems, cockscomb and perilla (shiso) herbs.

Serves 6

For the broth
5 litres (169 fl oz/21 cups) water
1.5 kg (3 lb 5 oz) free-range pork knuckle,
    trotter or bones
1.5 kg (3 lb 5 oz) grass-fed, free-range beef short rib
2 large oxtail chunks
1 tbsp sea salt
60 g (2 oz) rock sugar
1 large onion, cut both ends to stand
6 lemongrass stalks, bashed
1 daikon (about 15 cm/6 in), halved
1–1½ tbsp shrimp paste
1–2 beef stock cubes (optional)
2–3 tbsp tomato purée (paste)
4–5 tbsp fish sauce
1 tbsp vegetable oil
½ garlic bulb, finely chopped
2 round shallots, sliced
4 lemongrass stalks, finely diced
½ tbsp chilli powder
1 tbsp chilli oil

For the garnish
2 spring onions (scallions), thinly sliced
8 Thai basil sprigs, stem removed
2 bird's eye chillies, sliced with or without seeds
40 g (1½ oz) beansprouts, raw or blanched
    in boiling water (optional)
8 sprigs of Vietnamese coriander (cilantro)/laksa
    leaf, stem removed (optional)
2 limes, sliced into wedges

For the noodles
80 g (3 oz) per serving rice vermicelli (1.6 mm),
    cooked to packet instructions

To get a clear broth, bring a large saucepan of half of the water to the boil, then submerge the meat and bones with a generous amount of salt. Bring back to the boil then cook for 5 minutes until a scum comes to the surface. Remove from the heat and drain. Discard all the water, wash the meat and clean the pot. Measure the fresh water into the pan and bring to the boil.

Heat a griddle pan without any oil and char the onion, bashed lemongrass stalks and daikon, then add them to the pot with the meat, bones, salt and rock sugar. Return to the boil, then cover and simmer for 2½ hours, removing any scum that surfaces.

While waiting for the broth to cook, prepare the other ingredients. Then remove the meat from the broth into a bowl of cold water. Leave to stand for 10 minutes, then drain and leave to cool.

Slice the rib meat into thin pieces (3 mm thick) and extract the meat from the oxtail. Set aside in an airtight container or cover with beeswax wrap. Add the shrimp paste, beef stock cubes, if using, the tomato purée and season with fish sauce. In another small frying pan (skillet), heat the oil, add the garlic, shallots, diced lemongrass and chilli powder and fry until browned, then add the chilli oil. Pour everything into the broth, return it to a simmer and continue to simmer for another 20 minutes uncovered.

Assemble all the bowls with noodles, garnish with spring onions, sliced onion, coriander and beansprouts. Top with slices of beef rib and oxtail. When ready to serve, bring the broth to the boil. Pour the boiling broth over the noodle bowls until everything is submerged. Squeeze the lime at the table and add extra herbs and chillies.

PORK UDON

BÁNH CANH THỊT HEO

This very simple noodle soup really hits the spot every time and is great for days when you want a soup but don't want to spend hours in the kitchen. There is something so comforting about thick noodles; they are almost luxuriously pillowy. Here, I use Japanese udon noodles for ease. Apart from the beautiful flavour of broth that free-range pork belly gives, the crispy fried shallots add so much to it and it makes you wonder how something so tiny can be so full of flavour! Plus the pleasing zing of lime juice brings everything together. If this becomes your mid-week household favourite, remember that it's an excellent base to add leftover vegetables or to whatever you have to hand.

Serves 4

400 g (14 oz) free-range pork belly, skin and excess fat removed
1.5 litres (52 fl oz/6¼ cups) water
1 white onion
10 cm (4 in) daikon
1 tsp sea salt
20 g (¾ oz) rock sugar
1 tsp chicken or pork powder (optional)
3 tbsp fish sauce

For the noodle bowls
200 g (7 oz) per serving udon noodles
30 g (1 oz) coriander (cilantro), sliced 1 cm (½ in) pieces
1 spring onion (scallion), sliced into 1 cm (½ in) pieces
Crispy Shallots (page 206)
1 red chilli, sliced
handful of green leaves, such as *kai lan*, mustard leaves, chard or beetroot leaves, blanched in boiling water, then drained
Fish Cakes (page 143) (optional)
freshly ground black pepper
juice of 1 lime

Put the pork in a large saucepan and add enough boiling water to submerge the meat. Leave to sit for 5 minutes, then drain and discard the water. Then cover the meat with the measured amount of fresh boiling water and add the onion, daikon, sea salt, rock sugar and chicken or pork seasoning, if using. Bring to the boil, then cover and cook for 1 hour, skimming off any scum that surfaces.

Remove the pork from the broth and leave to cool at room temperature. Slice thinly. Remove the daikon and slice up to serve or discard. Add the fish sauce to the broth and cook for a further 5 minutes.

Cook the noodles as described on page 202, or according to the packet instructions.

Place the noodles into bowls with the toppings of coriander, spring onion, crispy shallots and chilli. Add the fish cakes, if using, plus the slices of pork belly, and decorate with some leaves of choice and a good seasoning of black pepper. When ready to serve, bring the broth to the boil and ladle it over the contents. Squeeze over a generous amount of lime juice and serve with fish sauce at the table, if required.

Note • If you don't have daikon, you can use kohlrabi or parsnip.

Make ahead Broth: 3–4 days
Herbs & noodles: 2–3 days

WATERCRESS, GINGER & PORK RIB SOUP

CANH SƯỜN XÀ LÁCH XOONG

This is a simple classic soup, usually served at the centre of the table for everyone to ladle out and share. It never fails to please a crowd with its light, refreshing and invigorating taste.

You can substitute the watercress with greens, such as mustard leaves, spinach, pea shoots, mugwort leaves and celery leaves. This soup is pretty versatile and it's delicious with any vegetables you may have kicking about, like marrow, courgettes (zucchini), squash and winter melon – just slice the vegetables thinly, add them near the end and cook until tender. For a more filling version, try the broth over some noodles or pasta. Add about 60 g (2 oz) of cooked noodles or pasta per person to a bowl and pour over the soup. If you don't have pork ribs, you can switch it out for a chicken carcass or the same weight in wings. Or use a vegetable stock and replace the fish sauce with salt to make a vegan version.

Serves 2

350 g (12 oz) free-range pork ribs
700 ml (24 fl oz/scant 3 cups) hot water
35 g (1¼ oz) ginger root, finely chopped
2 tbsp fish sauce
100 g (3½ oz) watercress
1 spring onion (scallion)

Wash the pork ribs by placing them in a bowl and immersing them in boiling water for a few minutes. Drain the water and repeat one more time.

Next, add the ribs to a saucepan with the hot water and ginger. Cover with a lid and bring to the boil over a medium heat, then cover and simmer for 20–30 minutes, or until tender.

When ready to serve, season with fish sauce and stir through the watercress until it wilts. Add the spring onion. I like to serve the soup in one big bowl with an array of other dishes and rice.

CHICKEN PHỞ

PHỞ GÀ

Easy to pull together, this is a favourite among the young, the old and everyone in between, all across the world. This is a much lighter fragrant *phở*. Among the Vietnamese, the rules are strict with the flavours of *phở* – but don't let that stop you. It is okay if you don't have all the spices, but it is important to have star anise.

Makes 4–5 bowls

2.5 litres (88 fl oz/10 cups) water or enough
    to cover the chicken
1 corn-fed, free-range chicken (about 1.5 kg/
    2 lb 4 oz)
1 large onion, cut at both ends to stand
150 g (5 oz) ginger root, halved
10 cm (4 in) daikon or parsnip (optional)
15 star anise (10–15 g/½ oz)
4 whole cloves
1 cinnamon stick
2 black cardamom pods (optional but good to have)
1 tbsp coriander seeds in a ball strainer or small
    muslin infuser
30 g (1 oz) rock sugar or 1 tbsp caster
    (superfine) sugar
15 g (½ oz/1 tbsp) sea salt
4 tbsp fish sauce (or more to taste)
1 chicken stock cube
75 g (2½ oz) dry flat rice noodles per serving
    or fresh *ho fun* noodles
freshly ground black pepper

For the garnish
coriander (cilantro) leaves, torn or coarsely chopped
3 spring onions (scallions), white and green parts,
    sliced lengthways, soaked in cold water until curled
1 red or white onion, thinly sliced
leaves from a few sprigs of Thai basil
    and/or sawtooth (if you can get it)
freshly ground black pepper
bird's eye chillies, sliced (optional)
lime wedges

Measure the water into a saucepan just large enough to hold the chicken and bring to the boil. Trim off any excess skin and fat around the cavity and neck of the chicken, then submerge in the boiling water. To achieve a clear broth, once the pot comes back to the boil, cover and simmer for 30 minutes, occasionally skimming off impurities.

In a griddle or frying pan (skillet) over a high heat, char the onion, ginger and daikon or parsnip on both sides, then add to the broth. Use the same pan to toast the spices until fragrant, then add them to the broth with the stock cubes, sugar and salt. Simmer for a further 30 minutes until the chicken is cooked.

Remove the chicken from the liquid and check that the juices run clear when you pierce the thigh. Set aside to cool. Remove the vegetables, bones and spices from the broth and discard. Separate the meat from the carcass and slice the chicken against the grain into bite-sized pieces.

Cook the noodles as described on page 202, or according to the packet instructions.

Divide the noodles among serving bowls. Place the sliced chicken on top, garnish with coriander, spring onion, red onion and basil leaves. Season with a pinch of pepper and a couple of slices of chilli, if using.

When ready to serve, season the broth with fish sauce, tasting with every spoonful to see if it's to your liking. Bring to the boil, then ladle the hot broth into the bowls, making sure that all the ingredients are submerged. Serve immediately with a squeeze of lime and more of the garnishes.

Note	• Substitute noodles with linguine or tagliatelle. Use leftover chicken in a salad.
Make ahead	Broth: 5 days Herbs & noodles: 2–3 days

CHICKEN, GINGER, MARROW & PUMPKIN NOODLE SOUP

NUI NẤU RAU CỦ

My mum used to make a version of this with carrots and potatoes when I felt poorly, but of course it can be enjoyed just as much when you're on top of the world. My daughter loves this refreshing and light soup – it always brings so much comfort. Use this recipe throughout the year with various vegetables and herbs according to the season.

Serves 2–3

2 chicken legs
1.2 litres (40 fl oz/4¾ cups) water
100 g (3½ oz) ginger root, sliced
1 small white onion
1 carrot
1 parsnip
1 celery stalk
2 tbsp fish sauce
15 g (½ oz) rock sugar
1 heaped tsp mushroom or chicken powder (optional)
250 g (9 oz) Delica pumpkin, peeled, seeds removed and flesh diced into 2.5 cm (1 in) cubes
250 g (9 oz) marrow, peeled, seeds removed and flesh diced into 2.5 cm (1 in) cubes
80 g (3 oz) per serving thin flat rice noodles (hủ tiếu) or macaroni
¾ tbsp groundnut (peanut) oil
2 round shallots, thinly sliced
4 garlic cloves, thinly sliced
1 spring onion (scallion), sliced diagonally 1 cm (½ in) thick
20 g (¾ oz) coriander (cilantro) leaves, roughly chopped
freshly ground black pepper
½ lemon, cut into wedges
red chillies, sliced (optional)

Put the chicken legs into a saucepan so they fit comfortably, submerge in boiling water, then leave for 5 minutes. Drain, discarding the water. Add the measured amount of fresh boiling water from the kettle, return to the boil, adding the ginger, onion, carrot, parsnip, celery stalk, fish sauce, rock sugar and mushroom or chicken powder, if using. Remove any scum that surfaces, then cover and simmer for 30 minutes.

Remove and discard all the vegetables except the ginger. Take out the chicken legs and set aside to rest and cool.

Add the pumpkin and marrow, cover and simmer for 15 minutes, or until soft but still holding their shape. Remove from the heat.

Cook the noodles as described on page 202, or according to the packet instructions. Add to a large soup bowl.

Heat the oil in a small frying pan (skillet) over a medium–low heat and fry the shallots until golden, then add the garlic and cook until golden and crisp. Then add the entire contents of the pan to the broth. Taste the broth and adjust the balance of flavours.

Remove the bones from the chicken legs and slice the meat against the grain into bite-sized pieces. Put on top of the noodles. Garnish with spring onion, coriander and plenty of black pepper. Add the pumpkin and marrow to the bowl.

When ready to serve, bring the broth to a bubbling boil, then ladle over the noodles in the bowl. Serve with lemon wedges and red chilli slices, if you like.

Make ahead — Broth, herbs & noodles: a few hours

HEAVENLY NOODLE SOUPS

DUCK & BAMBOO NOODLE SOUP

BÚN MĂNG VỊT

Serving bamboo is a traditional way of wishing all to be well. Bamboo is a sign of strength, harmony and luck, which is why it is often served at dinner parties. You normally dip the meat and cabbage salad in the sweet and fiery ginger sauce.

Serves 4

For the broth
1 tsp sea salt
4 duck legs, drumstick and thigh
80 g (3 oz) ginger root, sliced
2 litres (70 fl oz/3 cups) water
1 onion
½ tbsp salt
20 g (¾ oz) rock sugar or light brown sugar

For the ginger dipping sauce - see page 209

For the onion pickle - see page 206

For the crispy shallots - see page 206

For the side salad
30 g (1 oz) Vietnamese coriander (cilantro) leaves,
    cut into pieces
30 g (1 oz) coriander (cilantro) stalks and leaves,
    roughly chopped
150 g (5 oz) white cabbage, thinly sliced

For the bamboo shoots
1 tbsp shallot oil or vegetable oil
1 garlic clove, finely chopped
500 g (1 lb 2 oz) tinned baby bamboo shoots, soaked
    in water for an hour, rinsed well, wring to dry
2½ tbsp fish sauce
1 tsp caster (superfine) sugar
1 tbsp Marmite
1½ tsp MSG or chicken powder
4 spring onions (scallions), white ends, whole, save
    the spring onion greens for garnishing

For the noodles
80 g (3 oz) per serving rice vermicelli (0.8 mm)
    (page 202)

To make the broth, rub salt onto the duck legs, then use a couple of ginger slices and rub it all over. Rinse the duck legs in tap water. Bring the measured water to a half boil, then submerge the legs with the remaining ginger slices, the onion, salt, rock sugar and Vietnamese coriander stems from the side salad. Bring to the boil, then cover and cook on a low simmer for 20–30 minutes, skimming off any scum that surfaces periodically.

Make the ginger dipping sauce, onion pickle and crispy shallots.

To make the side salad, add half Vietnamese coriander and coriander into the bowl and mix half the onion pickle with the cabbage.

To cook the bamboo shoots, add the oil used to fry shallots or vegetables to the pan with garlic and gently fry until golden. Then add the bamboo shoots and stir-fry with the fish sauce, sugar, Marmite and MSG or chicken powder, if using, for 5 minutes.

After 20–30 minutes, remove the duck legs and place in a cold water bath for 10 minutes, then drain and set aside to rest. Remove the onion, ginger and Vietnamese coriander stems from the broth pot. With a ladle, remove and discard any excess fat. Transfer the stir-fried bamboo shoots into the broth and continue to simmer for 10–15 minutes with four white ends of spring onion. Then remove the bamboo and set aside.

Cook and drain the noodles as descrbed on page 202, or according to the packet instructions. Place the vermicelli into noodle soup bowls.

Take the meat off the bones, leaving the skin on, and cut against the grain into 1 cm (¾ in) thick slices. Place half onto the noodle bowls with some of the pickled onion and coriander, the green parts of spring onion, the bamboo and 1 tsp of the fried crispy golden shallots.

Serve the other half of the sliced duck on a bed of onion pickle and thinly sliced cabbage mixed with the other half of the Vietnamese coriander and coriander on a separate plate. When ready to serve, bring the broth to the boil, ladle the hot broth over the noodles and serve with extra herbs on the side, a squeeze of lime and a sprinkling of chillies. Serve each bowl of soup with the dipping sauce to dip the duck meat from the soup.

<u>Make ahead</u>   Broth, herbs & noodles: 1 day

FISH CAKE NOODLE SOUP

MÌ CHẢ CÁ

This is a simple and quick technique to make soup; it is easy to adapt with many seasonal ingredients. Watercress instils the broth with the most refreshing, peppery flavours, balancing well with the zing of ginger. Fried shallots and garlic add a sweet complexity to the broth, while the samphire adds a crunch as well as its salty seaside flavours. This is a fish cake recipe and a fish cake broth recipe. Here, I've made extra fish cakes for another meal, perfect in *bánh mì* (page 114) or with steamed rice, a lovely *nước mắm* (page 209) and plenty of vegetable sides and pickles.

Makes about 16 fish cakes

For the fish cakes
500 g (1 lb 2 oz) fish such as salmon and haddock, cut into 2.5 cm (1 in) chunks
1½ tbsp fish sauce
1 spring onion (scallion), roughly chopped
1 shallot, roughly chopped
3 garlic cloves, roughly chopped
20 g (¾ oz) dill fronds or coriander (cilantro) leaves, roughly chopped
1 Thai red chilli, sliced (optional)
zest of 1 lime, finely chopped
3 tbsp sunflower oil, for frying

For the broth
1.5 litres (52 fl oz/6¼ cups) boiling water
30 g (1 oz) ginger root, julienned, then finely chopped
3 tbsp fish sauce
2 tbsp vegetable oil
2 round shallots, sliced
2 garlic cloves, finely chopped

For the noodle bowls
4 nests of fine egg noodles
200 g (7 oz) watercress, shared between 4 bowls
1 spring onion (scallion), sliced
20 g (¾ oz) dill fronds, chopped
pinch of freshly ground black pepper
handful of samphire (or fine tip asparagus)

To make the fish cakes, put all the ingredients except the oil into a food processor and briefly pulse to blend together so you still retain some texture. If you don't have a small food processor, chop the fish and all the ingredients quite finely, put in a bowl and beat them together, mixing in one direction.

Lightly grease a plate or tray with 1 tablespoon of the oil and grease your hands. Take a lump of the fish cake mixture and form a patty with your hands, about 4 cm (1½ in) in diameter and place on the greased plate. Repeat with the remaining mixture to make about 16 fish cakes.

Heat the remaining oil in a large frying pan (skillet) over a medium–high heat and fry the fish cakes for about 3–4 minutes until golden on both sides. I usually start by placing one fish cake in the pan at 12 o'clock, then add them to the pan clockwise so I know which ones to turn, then remove and set aside. Keep the frying pan handy.

To make the broth, measure the boiling water into a saucepan and add the ginger and fish sauce. Add eight fried fish cakes, cover and simmer to let the ginger infuse for 7–10 minutes.

In the same frying pan used to fry the fish cakes, heat the oil over a medium heat and fry shallots until golden brown without letting them burn. Then add the garlic and watch until it turns golden, then remove from the pan and set aside.

Cook the noodles as described on page 202, or according to the packet instructions. Divide into bowls with the watercress, spring onion, a pinch of dill, pepper, samphire, fried golden shallots and garlic and fish cakes from the pot. Bring the broth to a boil, then ladle hot broth onto each bowl. This will poach the samphire and seep into the fish cakes, and the watercress will flavour the broth. Serve immediately.

Make ahead Fish cakes: 2 days
       Broth, herbs & noodles: Morning

TOMATO, EGG, CRAB
& TIGER PRAWN NOODLE SOUP

BÚN RIÊU CUA

There are many versions of this soup and everyone will have a different way to make it – some versions can take the entire day, but I find that making a quick *bún riêu* still hits the spot. You can add many things to this – such as fried tofu, Fish Cakes (page 143), Vietnamese ham or an array of beautiful fresh seafood! You can use whatever leaves and herbs you like – I usually go for a mix of things like celery leaves, mint, Vietnamese coriander (cilantro), cockscomb, perilla (shiso), Thai basil and coriander (cilantro).

Serves 4

1 tbsp vegetable oil
2 round shallots, sliced
4 garlic cloves, finely chopped
500 g (1 lb 2 oz) free-range pork bones, such as ribs
3 litres (100 fl oz/12½ cups) boiling water
50 g (2 oz) dried shrimps, soaked in warm water
    for 10 minutes, then drained
30 g (1 oz) rock sugar
2 tbsp tomato purée (paste)
200 g (7 oz) cherry tomatoes
4 whole tiger prawns
3 tbsp fish sauce
1 tbsp shrimp paste
juice of 1 lime

For the crab & eggs
4 eggs
200 g (7 oz) crab meat (fresh or tinned)
1 tbsp fish sauce
pinch of freshly ground black pepper
1 tsp caster (superfine) sugar

For the noodles
80 g (3 oz) per serving rice vermicelli (0.8 mm)

For the garnish
4 lime wedges
2 bird's eye chillies, thinly sliced, with or without seeds
chilli oil, to drizzle (optional)
a good selection of leaves and herbs

Heat the oil in a small frying pan over a medium–low heat and fry the shallots until golden, then add the garlic and fry until just browned. Set aside in a bowl.

To make a clear broth, submerge the bones in boiling water in a large saucepan, then allow them to sit for a couple of minutes. Drain and repeat. Clean the pan, return the meat to the pan and fill with the measured amount of boiling water. Then bring the ribs to a simmer over a medium heat.

Add the prepared shrimps, the rock sugar and tomato purée, cover and cook for 20 minutes. Add the cherry tomatoes, cover and continue to simmer for a further 10 minutes. Add the fish sauce and shrimp paste. Burst most of the tomatoes so that the juices seep into the broth.

In a separate bowl, beat the eggs and crab meat together with fish sauce, black pepper and sugar.

Remove the bones from the broth. Bring it back to a gentle boil and create a whirlpool in the pot by turning the broth around vigorously with cooking chopsticks or a wooden spoon. Slowly pour in the egg and crab mixture. Stop stirring once all the mixture is in the broth and let it sit. The egg mixture will cook and form clumps that will float to the top.

Add the tiger prawns, fried shallots and garlic. Cook over a medium–high heat for 5 minutes, then remove the prawns. Finally add the lime juice.

Cook the noodles as described on page 202, or according to the packet instructions.

Divide the noodles, egg, prawns and tomatoes between four bowls. Bring the broth to the boil, then ladle it over the noodle mixture, garnishing with herbs, chillies and a squeeze of lime, as desired.

Make ahead   Broth, herbs & noodles: morning

WONTON NOODLE SOUP

MÌ HOÀNH THÁNH

This originated from the many Chinese immigrants who have lived in Vietnam, and having Chinese food is a real treat. This is a mixture of a traditional and hybrid Vietnamese/Chinese/British recipe. I've added MSG to this recipe because it is the best way to provide the deep umami flavour it needs. If you don't want to use it, Marmite really does the trick. There are a lot of toppings you can choose to add to the soup, such as Roast Barbecued Pork (page 101).

Makes 24 wontons to serve 4

For the broth
1 white onion
5 round shallots
1 kg (2 lb 4 oz) pork bones or pork hand/knuckle
500 g (1 lb 2 oz) chicken wings or carcass
3 litres (100 fl oz/12½ cups) water
40 g (1½ oz) dried shrimp, soaked in warm water for 30 minutes, then drained and rinsed
20 g (¾ oz) rock sugar
½ tbsp sea salt
saved prawn heads from the wonton, if any
1 tsp MSG or 1 tbsp chicken powder or Marmite

For the wontons
100 g (3½ oz) king prawns, peeled and de-veined, reserving the heads for the broth, then finely chopped
80 g (3 oz) minced (ground) pork
50 g (2 oz) Jerusalem artichoke, finely chopped
1 spring onion (scallion), thinly sliced
1½ tbsp oyster sauce
pinch of sea salt
½ tsp caster (superfine) sugar
¼ tsp freshly ground black pepper
2 tsp sesame oil
½ tbsp cornflour (cornstarch), plus extra for dusting
1 pack 10 cm (4 in) square wonton wrappers
1 egg, beaten, for sealing

For the toppings
80 g (3 oz) per serving fresh thin egg noodles or flat rice noodles

60 g (2 oz) per serving of Roast Barbecued Pork (page 101) (optional)
2 tbsp Crispy Shallots (page 206)
2 spring onions (scallions), thinly sliced
40 g (1½ oz) garlic chives, sliced into 3 cm (1 in) lengths
40 g (1½ oz) coriander (cilantro) leaves, torn
2 red chillies, sliced diagonally (optional)
freshly ground black pepper to taste
chilli oil or chilli sauce (optional)

Preheat the oven to 200°C (400°F/gas 8). Put the whole onion and shallots in the oven and roast for 30 minutes until tender.

To make a clear broth, put the pork bones or knuckle, wings or carcass in a large saucepan, submerge in boiling water for 5 minutes, then drain and discard the water. Wash the pan and return it to the heat with the measured water and bring to the boil. Add the pork and bones, the dried shrimp, roasted onions and shallots. Season with rock sugar, salt and MSG, if using, or an alternative. Cover and cook for 2 hours over a medium–low heat, occasionally skimming the surface to remove any scum. Add the prawn heads as soon as you have prepared the wonton filling.

If using pork hand or knuckle, remove it from the broth and lower into a bowl of cold water for 10 minutes, then drain and leave to cool. If you are only using pork bones, remove the carcass or wings, bones, prawn heads and onions out of the stock, save any meat to add to the soup or another dish and discard the rest.

While the broth is cooking, make the wonton filling. Combine all the filling ingredients in a bowl and whip, stirring in one direction only, until the filling becomes a sticky-like paste.

Lightly dust a plate with cornflour. To form the dumplings, place a wrapper onto the palm of your hand and dollop 1 teaspoon of filling in the middle. Moisten the edges of the wrapper with the beaten egg. Fold the wonton wrapper over into a triangle, while pushing the air out of the filling, then pinch the wrapper together to form 'gold sacks' – seal by pinching and put them on the prepared plate. Repeat until you have used all the filling to make 24 wontons.

Notes
+ You can use tinned water chestnuts instead of Jerusalem artichoke.
+ Leftover meat can be used in summer rolls or salads.

Make ahead
Filling: 2 days
Cooked wontons: 2–3 days
Broth: 4–5 days
Herbs & noodles: 2 days

To cook the wontons, bring a pan of water to the boil, drop in a few wontons at a time so they fit the pan but don't crowd it, maintaining the boil. When they float, cook them for a further 2 minutes, then they are done. Lift them out of the water and repeat until you have cooked as many as you need. Keep any extras for later or freeze them.

Cook the noodles as described on page 202, or according to the packet instructions.

In each bowl, place some cooked noodles, cooked wontons and barbecued pork, if using. Garnish with crispy shallots, spring onions, garlic chives, coriander, chillies, if using, and black pepper.

Return the broth to the boil and ladle into the bowls. Serve immediately with an option of chilli oil or chilli sauce to serve.

6 QUICK MIDWEEK MEALS

It's good to have a varied stock of noodles, rice and pasta to throw together with what's in the fridge and any leftovers. Having broth is always helpful to whip up a real healthy instant noodle soup quickly too.

When I can, I dry out a batch of easy homemade noodles (page 205) and store them in a box for future uses with whatever fresh or storecupboard ingredients that are available. Then all you need to do is shake up a good sauce and you're almost there. Noodles fuel us so well with their versatile shapes, sizes and texture – they champion lovely sauces, plenty of vegetables and herbs, and make meat-free meals enjoyable and delightful.

The recipes in this chapter are easily adaptable so swap out with what you have and follow the main principle of the sauce and cooking method. They are delicious in a feast or eaten solo and popular with young children too (leaving out chilli). Feel free to leave out any meat or seafood and make vegetarian meals or adapt and re-invent leftovers. This is a guide to help you in the kitchen. Prepare everything before you cook; even lay the table because it will be quick.

STIR-FRIED BEEF & ASPARAGUS WITH FLAT RICE NOODLES

PHỞ XÀO THỊT BÒ MĂNG TÂY

For sharing or going solo. If you do not have fresh flat rice noodles, it is delicious with rice or any kind of packet pasta. You can use all sorts of crunchy greens, like sugar snap peas, mangetout (snow peas), chayote, kale, chard, courgette (zucchini), fine green beans or runner beans.

Serves 2

200 g (7 oz) ribeye, sirloin or rump steak, cut into
    1 cm (½ in) thick slices

For the marinade
1 garlic clove, finely chopped
1 tbsp oyster sauce
1 tbsp soy sauce
1 tsp maple syrup
freshly ground black pepper

For the noodles
160 g (6 oz) fresh *ho fun* noodles, separated, or dry
    rice noodles or Fresh Homemade Egg Noodles
    (page 205)
2 tbsp vegetable oil
1 onion, sliced, 1 cm (¾ in) thick
200 g (7 oz) asparagus, sliced lengthways into
    10 cm (4 in) pieces
100 ml (2½ fl oz/scant ½ cup) water or *phở* broth
2 tbsp oyster sauce
2 tbsp soy sauce
100 g (3½ oz) beansprouts
freshly ground black pepper

Mix together the marinade ingredients and marinate the beef for 20 minutes.

Cook the noodles as described on page 202, or according to the packet instructions.

Heat a large frying pan (skillet) over a high heat until very hot, then add 1 tablespoon of vegetable oil and then add half the onion and stir-fry for 1 minute. Add the steak, let it sit for 30 seconds before shaking it and stirring it, searing on both sides. Add the asparagus, 1 tablespoon of oyster sauce, a splash of water (or *phở* broth) and stir-fry for a couple of minutes or until the steak is cooked as you like it. Then remove from the heat and set aside on a plate to rest.

Heat the same frying pan or wok to a high heat again with 1 tablespoon of oil, add the rest of the onions, stirring quickly, then add the noodles, 1 tablespoon of oyster sauce and soy sauce and stir well for a couple of minutes. Add beansprouts and a dash of water or *phở* broth and stir-fry for a further 1 minute until the noodles or pasta are soft. Pour onto a serving plate. Add the beef and asparagus to the noodles and serve.

LANGOUSTINES POACHED IN COCONUT WATER WITH SAMPHIRE

TÔM HÙM HẤP NƯỚC DỪA

To accompany a noodle dish or indulge as a blissful treat on its own with some dips. Much of Vietnam is coastal and seafood is plentiful. Nosily sharing a plate of shellfish and crustaceans serves as great finger-licking entertainment with a friend or two.

Serves 2

For the ginger sauce
3 cm (1 in) piece ginger root, finely grated
1 tsp chilli sauce
2 tbsp fish sauce
zest of 1 lime
2 tbsp lime juice (1–2 limes)
1 tbsp light brown sugar
1 tbsp sesame oil
a few coriander (cilantro) stalks, chopped

For the cider vinegar sauce
2 tbsp cider vinegar or lime or lemon juice
1 tsp freshly ground black pepper
½ round shallot, finely chopped
1 tsp caster (superfine) sugar

For the langoustines
500 ml (17 fl oz/2 cups) coconut water
8 langoustine, cleaned, left whole
200 g (7 oz) samphire
1 lemon or lime, quartered

To prepare the dipping sauces, mix the ingredients together in separate bowl. Set aside.

Bring the coconut water to a boil, then add the langoustines, cover and cook for 1 minute, then turn to cook all the sides for about 30–60 seconds. When they are a paler pink, they are done. Set aside.

Meanwhile, bring a kettle of water to the boil, pour over the samphire and blanch for 20 seconds. Drain well.

Plate up the langoustines and samphire with the sauces and wedges of lemon or lime. It is also really good with vegetarian glass noodles (page 202).

SAVOY CABBAGE, ROASTED CAULIFLOWER & CASHEW CHILLI NOODLES

MÌ XÀO CHAY

I really love British vegetables and if I have the luxury of time to make fresh, homemade noodles, I would make it just so I could have a portion of this dish – so delicious and as easy to make as a regular pasta. There is something so moreish and savoury about butter and fish sauce which turns this midweek dinner into a real treat. Get everything prepped beforehand and stir-fry at the last minute before serving.

Serves 2

250 g (9 oz) cauliflower, sliced into 1 cm (¾ in) thick florets
½ tbsp vegetable oil
¼ tsp sea salt
2 tbsp fish sauce
1 tbsp chilli (hot pepper) flakes
1 tbsp maple syrup
300 g (½ oz) Fresh Homemade Egg Noodles (page 205) or dried or store bought
1½ tsp sesame oil
30 g (1 oz) butter
2 round shallots, halved and sliced into rings
3 garlic cloves, sliced
100 g (3½ oz) Savoy cabbage, sliced into 1 cm (½ in) strips
20 g (¾ oz) coriander (cilantro), roughly chopped
handful of cashews, roughly chopped
lime wedges, to serve

Preheat the oven to 200°C (400°F/gas 8).

Roast the cauliflower with a brush of vegetable oil and a sprinkling of salt for 20–25 minutes.

Mix the fish sauce, chilli flakes and maple syrup in a jar or bowl.

Cook the noodles as described on page 202, or according to the packet instructions. Fresh noodles will take 2 minutes, dried about 6 minutes. Drain and rinse with warm running water. Toss with the sesame oil.

Meanwhile, melt the butter in a large frying pan (skillet) over a low heat. Add the shallots and cook for 3 minutes, or until translucent. Turn the heat up to high, then add the garlic, cabbage and 3–4 tablespoons of pasta water and stir-fry for 2 minutes before adding the roasted cauliflower. Fry for 2 minutes. Add the cooked pasta to the frying pan with coriander. Pour the fish sauce, chilli and maple syrup around the pan, stir-fry and toss to cook for a further 3 minutes, then turn off the heat.

Serve with a generous sprinkling of chopped cashews and finish with a squeeze of lime.

FRIED NOODLES & GREENS

MÌ CHAY XÀO RAU

There are so many things you can do with this recipe to adapt it – work with whatever you have to hand and use up fresh and storecupboard ingredients. Feel free to use any combination of green leaves, cut into bite-sized pieces. It is really quick and easy, so prepare everything first so you are ready to go, then be prepared to work fast. Instead of lemongrass you can also use ginger or just garlic and shallots. This is also great as a cold noodle lunch or picnic.

Serves 2

1 round shallot, sliced
1 lemongrass stalk, finely chopped
1½ tbsp vegetable oil
1 garlic clove, crushed
200 g (7 oz) or a handful of green leaves such
   as Chinese mustard leaf, Chinese broccoli,
   choi sum, pak choi, kale, chard, cavolo nero
   or even tenderstem broccoli, hard stems
   removed, roughly sliced
2 nest dry egg noodles
5 tbsp noodle water

For the sauce
2 tbsp soy sauce
2 tbsp lime or lemon juice
finely chopped zest of 1 lime
1 tbsp maple syrup
2 tsp sesame oil

For the garnish
spring onions (scallions), coriander (cilantro),
   Thai basil, mint
plenty of chilli oil, to taste
nuts such as pistachios, peanuts, cashews,
   pine nuts, coarsely chopped

Prepare all the ingredients first. Put the shallot, lemongrass and oil in a frying pan (skillet), not yet on the heat. Mix all the sauce ingredients together, then set aside.

Cook the noodles as described on page 202, or according to the packet instructions. Drain, reserving a little of the noodle water, and rinse with warm running water. Drain and cover until needed.

Heat the frying pan and gently fry until the shallots and lemongrass are slightly golden. Turn the heat to medium. Add the greens and garlic with a dash of the reserved noodle water. Cook until wilted and tender, about 2 minutes or less. If using broccoli, give it 5 minutes.

Add the noodles then the sauce. Using cooking chopsticks or two utensils, stir and mix well together for a minute or until combined. Serve immediately with the garnishes.

SINGAPORE FRIED NOODLES WITH PURPLE SPROUTING BROCCOLI

BÚN XÀO SINGAPORE

This is great as part of a feast, weekend brunch or a midweek special. Swap out broccoli for any other seasonal vegetables or herbs.

Serves 2

For the sauce
1 tsp caster (superfine) sugar
1 tbsp soy sauce
1 tbsp oyster sauce
2 tsp sesame oil

For the omelette
2 eggs, beaten
1 spring onion (scallion), sliced diagonally
    1 cm (½ in) thick
pinch of caster (superfine) sugar
pinch of freshly ground black pepper
1 tsp soy sauce
1 tsp vegetable oil
1 small round shallot, sliced

For the noodles
2 tbsp oil, for frying
½ bird's eye chilli or 1 whole red chilli, finely chopped
2 round shallots, roughly chopped
10 dried shrimp, soaked in boiling water for
    10–15 minutes until soft, then drained (optional)
70–100 g (3–3½ oz) purple sprouting broccoli,
    sliced, bite-sized
150 g (5 oz) fine rice vermicelli (0.8 mm), soaked in
    cold water for 5 minutes, then drained
100 g (3½ oz) beansprouts
1½ tbsp Vietnamese curry powder (or mild, medium
    curry – your choice)
100 g (3½ oz) cooked king prawns
100 g (3½ oz) Roast Barbecued Pork (page 101),
    roughly chopped (optional)
20 g (¾ oz) garlic chives, cut into 5 cm (2 in) pieces
freshly ground black pepper

Mix together the sauce ingredients and set aside.

In a small bowl, combine all the omelette ingredients except the shallots. Set aside. In a large frying pan (skillet) or wok, gently fry the shallots with a dash of oil over a medium heat until golden, then pour the egg mixture over and fry until set. Remove from the pan, slice into 1 cm (½ in) strips and set aside.

Place the same pan back over a medium heat, pour in 1 tablespoon of oil and fry the chopped chilli, shallots and dried shrimp together for a minute until soft. Then turn to a high heat, adding the purple sprouting broccoli and continue to fry for a further 3 minutes, shaking the pan and charring the edges.

Still on a high heat, add the beansprouts for 30 seconds, then the noodles, mix together and stir-fry for a couple of minutes. Pour in the sauce ingredients and evenly sprinkle with the curry powder, covering the noodles all over and mixing well together for 2 minutes. Add the omelette to the pan with the cooked prawns and continue stir-frying for a further 3 minutes, or until the noodles are soft. Turn off the heat and mix in the garlic chives. Season with black pepper and serve immediately.

Notes
- Use any leftover cooked meat in the noodles.
- If you want to cook raw prawns or other types of seafood, such as mussels, clams or scallops, gently fry them in some garlic and a pinch of salt first, then add to the stir-fried noodles.

HOMEMADE NOODLES, TOMATOES & BROCCOLI

MÌ Ý XÀO RAU XANH

Here, I have used homemade pasta as I like to have a batch in the storecupboard ready to use. You can use store-bought pasta, too, or egg noodles. Adapt this recipe using any green leaves or vegetables, and make use of a variety of winter and summer leaves, such as Chinese broccoli leaves (*kai lan*), celery leaves, horseradish leaves and kale. The idea is to use the starchy cooking water and butter to make the sauce cling onto the noodle strands, making it luxurious and mouthwateringly good. You can also consider garnishing it with lots of herbs, too, add cold cuts or leftover roasted vegetables. Adapt this dish to the seasons and what is available to you.

Serves 2

2 tbsp fish sauce or soy sauce
1 tsp cider vinegar
1 tsp caster (superfine) sugar
150 g (5 oz) Fresh Homemade Egg Noodles (page 205)
pinch of sea salt
1 tbsp vegetable oil
2 round shallots, finely diced
2 garlic cloves, peeled, whole, crushed with a knife
100 g (3½ oz) tenderstem broccoli, sliced into bite-sized pieces
100 g (3½ oz) tomatoes, quartered
20 g (¾ oz) butter
20 g (¾ oz) Parmesan, grated
4 tsp chilli oil with shrimp (optional)
Crispy Shallots (page 206) (optional)
chilli (hot pepper) flakes to season (optional)

In a small bowl, mix together the soy sauce, cider vinegar and sugar. Set aside. Bring a saucepan of water to the boil with a generous pinch of salt, add the homemade noodles and cook for about 2–3 minutes until al dente (or or according to packet instructions if using pasta).

Meanwhile, in a large hot frying pan (skillet), add a dash of vegetable oil and fry the shallots and garlic until golden brown. Add the chopped tenderstem broccoli and tomatoes, and mix in the soy sauce mixture. After about 3–5 minutes, add half a mug of noodle water to the frying pan, then add the butter and Parmesan. Mix well together for 2 minutes. Take the noodles out of the pan with a pair of tongs and put them in the frying pan, then add 2–3 tablespoons of the noodle water and mix through until all the strands are covered with sauce. Toss well together. Place on serving plates with chilli oil, crispy shallots and chilli flakes, if using.

GLASS NOODLES WITH VEGETABLES

MIẾN XÀO

Korean *japchae* is slippery, smooth and succulent. It is usually stir-fried with beef on special occasions, but I love a vegetarian version just as much. Feel free to add strips of omelette, leftover roast chicken, roasted fish or slices of fried tofu. It is also great to use any type of nước mắm (pages 208–209) in the cooking.

Serves 2

For the sauce
2 bird's eye chillies, finely chopped
2 tbsp soy sauce
2 tbsp oyster sauce or mushroom sauce
1½ tbsp maple syrup
pinch of freshly ground black pepper

For the noodles
200 g (7 oz) (Korean) sweet potato noodles, soaked
    in boiling water for 10 minutes, covered
1 tbsp groundnut (peanut) or avocado oil
1 tsp sesame oil
1 tbsp vegetable oil
2 round shallots, sliced
2 garlic cloves, finely chopped
200 g (7 oz) courgette (zucchini), julienned
    or grated
200 g (7 oz) carrot, julienned
100 g (3½ oz) fennel, thinly sliced
100 g (3½ oz) beansprouts
50 g (2 oz) garlic chives, cut into 5 cm (2 in) pieces
splash of chicken stock or water
50 g (2 oz) pistachios, roughly chopped
    and lightly toasted

For the garnish
any herb (optional)
chilli oil or chilli sauce (optional)

In a small bowl, mix together the sauce ingredients and set aside.

Once the noodles have soaked, drain them, snip them roughly into 15–20 cm (6–8 in) lengths using scissors and then toss with 1 tablespoon of groundnut or avocado oil, sesame oil and half of the sauce mixture so that all the strands get a coating.

Place the prepared vegetables around a plate starting from 12 o'clock in the order they will cook – shallots, garlic, courgette, beansprouts and finally the chives.

Heat a medium frying pan (skillet) or wok over a medium heat, add ½ tablespoon of the vegetable oil and fry half the shallots until golden, then add half the garlic and fry until fragrant and golden, then add the carrots and cook for 2 minutes. Add the courgettes and cook for 2 minutes. Add the other half of the sauce, then add the beansprouts and finally the chives. Stir-fry vigorously for a minute until everything is slightly wilted. Set aside on a plate.

Starting again in the same pan over a medium-high heat, add ½ tablespoon of vegetable oil and fry the rest of the shallots, then the garlic as above. When golden, add the noodles and fry vigorously for about 4–5 minutes until the noodles flatten and turn soft, adding a dash of chicken stock or water to steam and to separate the noodles. They should be wet and slippery. Remove from the heat and mix together with the vegetables, sprinkle with pistachios and extra herbs, if using, onto a big platter to share.

7 SWEET THINGS

Sweet things are really popular in Vietnamese culture. Vietnamese people give gifts of sweet things and treats all the time, both to themselves and those they love. *Chè* is the most popular; it is like bubble tea or a sweet soup, made from many colourful and textural root vegetables, fresh and dried fruit, a variety of beans and grains, tapioca, herbal jellies, seaweed and nuts. It can be quite a healthy and refreshing treat.

In this chapter, I have included many baked goods that you could bring as gifts and win affection. Home ovens are quite scarce in Vietnam so anything that is baked is regarded as unique, skilled and very French.

My trips to Vietnam are defined by late-night strolls along the Honda-littered streets of my mum's hometown of Phan Thiết. Going to eat crème caramel or *chè* is an evening event in itself, a time to be exuberant over stories and lively discussions. All roads lead to dark, perfumed jasmine gardens, lit by strings of fairy lights, infested with high-pitched mosquitoes, cricket ambiance and faint songs of love and sorrow. The hosts bring out the best slices of sweet baked custardy crème caramel underneath a small mountain of crushed ice with coffee poured over it. Sundae glasses are filled with layers of white coconut milk, yellow sweet mung bean paste, green pandan jelly, purple sweet stewed beans and crushed ice.

I can't get enough of it, so I have used pandan in a few recipes. Pandan is a popular aromatic ingredient. It is a grassy tropical shrub, the vanilla of the Far East. Its unique and irresistible flavour is often used in desserts as well as in savoury dishes. Pandan cake is often a gift you'd receive when someone visits, much like bringing a bottle.

CRÈME CARAMEL

BÁNH KEM CARAMEL

This French dish has become the most Vietnamese of all Vietnamese desserts. The secret here is using condensed milk, which is a storecupboard essential.

You'll need a 25-cm (10-in) pie dish, as well as a deep baking tray for a bain-marie for this recipe. You can also use individual ramekins and steam the custard instead.

Serves 6–8

For the crème
2 egg yolks
4 eggs
120 ml (4 fl oz) double (heavy) cream
200 g (7 oz) condensed milk
250 ml (8 fl oz) milk
1½ tsp vanilla extract

For the caramel
110 g (3¾ oz/½ cup) caster (superfine) sugar
2 tbsp water

Preheat the oven to 160°C (320°F/gas 4).

Beat the egg yolks and eggs together in a large mixing bowl, then add the rest of the crème ingredients and stir to combine.

To make the caramel, sprinkle the sugar evenly into the bottom of a saucepan with 2 tablespoons of water over a low heat and leave it to sit without stirring. After about 5 minutes, the sides will start to turn into liquid and bubble but leave it to sit and resist the urge to stir. After about 12 minutes a quarter of the sugar will start to brown, so shake and swivel the pan and wait a further few minutes until it is mostly liquid and golden. Turn off the heat and continue to swivel until all the sugar has caramelised and turned a rich golden colour. Quickly pour a thin layer of caramel into the pie dish, just enough to cover the bottom and swirl very quickly (as it will harden) to cover all the edges and some along the sides and leave a few minutes to set. Tap it with a spoon to check for hardness.

Place the pie dish into a deep roasting tin, pour the crème mixture into the dish then fill the tray halfway with boiling water to form a bain-marie.

Bake for 25–30 minutes. To check if it is cooked, gently jiggle the dish – it should wobble tightly and evenly. Once it's set, leave to cool and refrigerate.

To serve, loosen the custard with a thin knife around the sides, place a serving plate over the dish, turn the dish upside down, tap out or shake once for the baked crème caramel to shift onto the plate. The caramel should drizzle down the sides.

PANDAN SWISS ROLL WITH MANGO & CREAM

BÁNH BÔNG LAN LÁ DỨA CUỘN NHÂN XOÀI

A light, fluffy cloud-like sponge is always well received especially if its flavoured with pandan leaves. Swiss rolls are a much-loved treat.

You can use the cake recipe in a standard baking tin and get the most gorgeous chiffon sponge (bake for 25–35 minutes or until a skewer comes out clean). If you can't get your hands on fresh pandan you can replace it with 1 teaspoon of pandan extract with 200 ml (7 fl oz/scant cup) of coconut water, available online or in Asian grocers. You can also replace the pandan in this recipe with just coconut milk or a fruit juice.

You will need a 30 x 30 cm (12 x 12 in), 2½-cm (1-in) deep baking sheet for this recipe or something similar.

Serves 6–8

For the swiss roll batter
100 g (3½ oz) pandan leaves, washed
200 ml (7 fl oz/scant 1 cup) coconut water
6 eggs, separated
110 g (1 cup) caster (superfine) sugar
200 ml (7 fl oz/scant 1 cup) vegetable oil
150 g (5 oz/1¼ cups) self-raising flour
1 heaped tsp baking powder

For the filling
1 mango, just ripe, destoned and chopped into 1 cm (½ in) cubes
200 ml (7 fl oz/scant 1 cup) double (heavy) cream
2 tbsp icing (confectioner's) sugar

Preheat the oven to 200°C (400°F/gas 8).

Blend the pandan leaves with the coconut water until smooth. Push the liquid through a sieve and into a bowl, making sure you squeeze out all the juice but discard any dry minced pandan.

Put the egg yolks in a big mixing bowl and the whites into a freestanding mixer bowl. To the bowl with the yolks, add the oil, flour, baking powder and 200 ml (7 fl oz) of pandan extract. Whisk together until it becomes smooth. Set aside.

Whisk the egg whites in the freestanding mixing bowl until soft peaks form. Slowly sprinkle in the sugar and whisk until the soft peaks are glossy, slightly firmer but not completely stiff.

With a spatula, spoon a big dollop of egg white into the yolk mixture bowl and mix well together. Then gently and lightly fold in the rest of the egg whites, a dollop at a time. Pour onto the prepared baking tray and bake for 12–15 minutes until springy to the touch. Leave to cool, then remove from the tray onto a work surface.

Meanwhile, whip the cream with the icing sugar until just forming soft peaks.

To assemble, spread an even layer of cream onto the brown side of the cake, then sprinkle over the mango cubes. Cut a clean sheet of baking parchment the same size as the baking tray and set it aside.

Using the baking parchment underneath to help you, start to slowly roll and fold the cake away from you, 3 cm (1 in) at a time, making sure the mango stays in while peeling away the paper as you roll. When you've reached the end, move the swiss roll onto the clean sheet of paper, roll it up, twisting the ends, then refrigerate for at least 2 hours.

Remove from the fridge when you are ready to eat it. Slice into 3 cm (1 in) rounds using a serrated knife. You can decorate with fruit or icing sugar, but it's just as delicious served plain.

PANDAN ICE CREAM

KEM LÁ DỨA

Pandan in everything, I say! Especially good in ice cream made ahead for instant after-dinner treats, served with shortbread or Pandan Swiss Roll (page 172).

If you don't have pandan, try a couple of vanilla beans with 40 g (1½ oz) grated ginger root or store-bought stem ginger, finely chopped.

Serves 6

80 g (3 oz) pandan leaves, cut into 10 cm (4 in) pieces
200 ml (7 fl oz/scant 1 cup) coconut water
200 g (7 oz) condensed milk
200 ml (7 fl oz/scant 1 cup) double (heavy) cream

Blend the pandan leaves with the coconut water until smooth. Push the liquid through a sieve and into a bowl, making sure you squeeze out all the juice but discard any dry minced pandan.

Mix together the pandan extract with the condensed milk and cream. Churn in an ice cream maker for 50 minutes, or according to the machine instructions. If you don't have an ice-cream maker, place the contents into a tub and freeze for 2 hours. Mash it up with a fork, then freeze again. Repeat once or twice more until the ice cream is frozen through.

CASSAVA CAKE

BÁNH KHOAI MÌ NƯỚNG

Many root vegetables, beans, seaweed and herbs are used in Vietnamese desserts for their medicinal benefits and vast availability. To peel cassava, use a sharp knife to pierce about 3 mm (⅛ in) deep. There is a layer of white skin just beneath the hairy brown skin. Buy a glossy fresh-looking cassava; sometimes the greengrocer can slice a bit off the tip to check if the cassava is fresh, pure white and has no black threads. Don't eat raw cassava as it can be poisonous. You can also buy frozen cassava, which is already grated. The coconut milk should be 70 per cent milk and 30 per cent water.

This recipe is courtesy of my old school friend Chriselia De Vries's mother, Delia Bermudez.

Serves 4

125 g (4 oz) butter
125 g (4 oz/scant ⅔ cup) caster (superfine) sugar
200 ml (7 fl oz/scant 1 cup) whole milk
400 ml (13 fl oz/generous 1½ cups) coconut milk
6 medium or large eggs, beaten
500 g (1 lb 2 oz) cassava, peeled and grated
400 g (14 oz) condensed milk

Preheat the oven to 180°C (350°F/gas 6) and place a 20 cm (8 in) baking dish on a baking sheet lined with baking parchment (in case the mixture spills over).

Melt the butter with the sugar, then pour the mixture into a large mixing bowl and add the milk, coconut milk, eggs and grated cassava. Stir it all together, then pour into the prepared baking dish and bake for 45 minutes, or until firm.

Remove from the oven and spread the condensed milk evenly over the top. Return to the oven for about 15–20 minutes, or until it is brown, caramelised and bubbling.

Serve at room temperature or chilled.

Notes
- Instead of cassava, you can use sweet potato, purple sweet potato, carrot or parsnip.

COCONUT RICE PUDDING WITH GINGER SYRUP & GRILLED PEACHES

CHÈ NẾP GỪNG TRÁI ĐÀO

Vietnamese rice pudding is usually cooked with black-eyed peas and it is so delicious! It can be served warm or cold with a pour of coconut cream and topped with any of your favourite fruits and berries. Sweet summer peaches and nectarines pair really well with ginger.

Serves 4

For the rice pudding
4 ripe, slightly firm peaches, stoned and halved
1 tsp coconut oil
100 g (3½ oz) glutinous rice, soaked for at least 30 minutes
500 ml (17 fl oz/2 cups) coconut water
30 g (1 oz) rock sugar
2 pandan leaves, tied into a small knot (optional)
400 g (14 oz) black-eyed peas, rinsed, drained

For the ginger syrup
(or you can just use stem ginger syrup from the jar)
100 g (3½ oz) palm sugar
50 g (2 oz) ginger root, sliced
about 3 tbsp water

For the coconut cream
100 ml (2½ fl oz/scant ½ cup) coconut cream
1 tsp caster (superfine) sugar (or to taste)
small pinch of sea salt (or to taste)
1 tsp cornflour (cornstarch) mixed to a smooth paste with 1 tbsp water

Heat a griddle pan over a high heat until hot. Brush the peaches with a little coconut oil, then place them cut-side down in the hot pan, grill for 3 minutes or when charred marks appear, then turn them over (they shouldn't be falling apart) and grill the skin side for a further 3 minutes. Set aside.

Gently cook the glutinous rice with coconut water and rock sugar for about 15 minutes, covered, until it has expanded and the sugar has dissolved. Add the pandan leaves, if using, and black-eyed peas and continue to simmer without the lid for another 5–10 minutes, stirring occasionally.

In a small pan, make the ginger syrup by adding all the ingredients together and simmering for 10–15 minutes.

In another small pan, add all the ingredients for the coconut cream, mix well to thicken and bring to a gentle boil, then remove from the heat.

Serve the rice pudding with grilled peaches, topped with coconut cream and ginger syrup.

Notes
- This is also lovely made with plums.

COCONUT & MANGO PUDDING WITH SAGO TAPIOCA BALLS

CHÈ DỪA XOÀI BỘT BÁNG

This is a type of *chè*, playful and colourful; it is like a sweet drink to lightly finish off the meal. Tapioca is made from cassava starch. This is a great one to make in advance – prepare it in the morning, then chill until ready to eat. Combine with mango or a mix of exotic fruit when ready to serve.

Serves 6–8

500 ml (17 fl oz/2 cups) coconut water
50 g (2 oz) rock sugar
1½ tbsp tapioca
60 g (2 oz) sago pearls
200 ml (7 fl oz/scant 1 cup) coconut milk
    (70 per cent milk/30 per cent water)
1 mango, peeled and diced

Bring the coconut water and rock sugar to the boil, then add the tapioca and sago balls. Simmer for about 5 minutes until the balls float to the top and the outer layer of the tapioca and sago become transparent (taste one to check if it is soft to the bite). Add the coconut milk, bring to the boil, then remove from the heat and leave to cool at room temperature before chilling in the fridge.

To serve, place cubed mango pieces in bowls or glasses and ladle in the pudding.

ORANGE & LIME BAKED CHEESECAKE

BÁNH PHÔ MAI CAM CHANH

The colour orange and the fruit symbolise good fortune and luck. Oranges are popular gifts. This recipe is based on a plain Japanese cheesecake, fluffy and wobbly. You can replace the orange juice and marmalade to make a plain cheesecake with vanilla and milk or add 150 ml (5 fl oz/scant ⅔ cup) fresh pandan extract (Pandan Swiss Roll, page 172).

You will need a lined cake tin and a larger roasting tin for a bain-marie for this recipe.

Serves 6–8

For bowl 1
120 ml (4 fl oz/½ cup) orange juice
225 g (8 oz) cream cheese
60 g (2 oz) unsalted butter
75 g (2½ oz) marmalade
6 egg yolks
zest and juice of 1 lime
85 g (3 oz/⅔ cup) self-raising flour
35 g (1¼ oz/⅓ cup) cornflour (cornstarch)
1 tsp baking powder

For bowl 2 – free-standing mixer bowl
6 eggs white
125 g (4 oz/heaped 12 cup) caster (superfine) sugar

Preheat the oven to 160°C (320°F/gas 4). Lightly grease a 20 cm (8 in) round cake tin and line with baking parchment.

Put the cream cheese and orange juice in a large heatproof bowl and place it over a saucepan of simmering water. Add the butter and stir frequently until melted and smooth. This should take about 5 minutes. Remove from the heat and cool completely for at least 15 minutes, then stir in the marmalade.

Sift the self-raising flour into another bowl with the baking powder and cornflour. Sift again into the cream cheese mixture, then mix well. Mix together the egg yolks and lime zest and lime juice. Set aside.

In a free-standing mixer, on a high speed, whip the egg whites until foamy, then slowly add the sugar, 1 tbsp at a time. Continue beating until the mixture forms glossy medium stiff peaks.

Take a big spoonful of whites and mix into the cream cheese bowl to combine, then lightly fold the rest of the egg whites into the cream cheese mixture.

Pour into the prepared cake tin. Place the tin inside a larger baking dish to create a bain-marie. Fill the large tin with hot water until it reaches halfway up the sides of the cake tin.

Bake in the preheated oven for about 1 hour 20 minutes until the cheesecake is set and golden brown on top. A skewer inserted in the centre should come out clean. Transfer to a wire rack to cool completely.

Decorate to your heart's desire, depending on the occasion, or serve plain. For example, make a lime frosting by mixing the icing sugar and lemon juice.

Note • You can make this in a bundt tin, in which case turn it upside down to cool.

Make ahead 2–3 days

CROISSANT PUDDING WITH COCONUT & BANANA

BÁNH CHUỐI NƯỚNG

Condensed milk is such a guilty pleasure! It does work in making so many things taste wonderful. Here it is used to bake croissants and replicates many things the Vietnamese love about the French cuisine. Throw in a bit of whisky for a special kick. Use up leftover croissants or baguette, ripe bananas and berries. If you can, use small Vietnamese bananas, which are more concentrated, sweet and not as flaky as Cavendish ones. When they are cooked, they become yet another element of deliciousness.

Serves 6–8

200 g (7 oz) condensed milk
400 ml (13 fl oz/generous 1½ cups) coconut cream, whisked to a smooth consistency. If cold, warm up until smooth in a pan
200 ml (7 fl oz/scant 1 cup) store-bought vanilla custard
good splash of whisky (optional)
4 medium croissants
6 ladyfinger or bananito (mini) bananas, sliced 5 mm (¼ in) thick or 2 Cavendish bananas
50 g (2 oz) milk chocolate, broken into 2-cm (¾-in) bits
50 g (2 oz) strawberries, sliced (optional)

Preheat the oven to 160°C (320°F/gas 4).

Mix together the condensed milk, coconut cream, custard and whisky, if using.

Tear the croissants into pieces and create a layer inside a 20 x 15-cm (8 x 6-in) baking dish. Cover with banana and chocolate chips. With a ladle, pour the mixture over to cover. Repeat until you have used all the ingredients, then place the strawberry slices on top.

Bake for 35 minutes until bubbling on the sides and golden on top. Serve hot or cold.

Note   • Substitute croissants with baguettes or sliced bread.

MATCHA CRÊPES WITH LIME CURD, PASSION FRUIT & FLAT PEACHES

BÁNH KẸP TRÀ XANH ĐÀO CHANH DÂY

This is very much like *bánh xèo* (page 84) in its technique but, of course, a sweet version. To me, Vietnam has become much more cosmopolitan than when I was a child. The influence of world foods and historical occupancy from the French, Japanese and Chinese has changed and sculpted the culinary landscape and diets to great extent. My combined love for British, French and Japanese cuisines are adapted here, resulting in a very satisfying dish.

Makes 6

For the lime and passion fruit curd
juice of 1 lime
2 passion fruits
50 g (2 oz) caster (superfine) sugar
30 g (1 oz) butter
1 egg, beaten

For the filling
3 peaches, de-stoned, then sliced into quarters
handful of strawberries, topped and quartered

For the crêpe batter
100 g (3⅓ oz/scant ⅔ cup) rice flour
   (Asian Rose Brand, or any non-glutinous)
1 heaped tsp matcha, mixed with 1 tbsp hot water
   until combined
200 ml (7 fl oz/scant 1 cup) coconut milk
   (50 per cent milk/50 per cent water)
200 ml (7 fl oz/scant 1 cup) water
zest of 1 lime
50 g (2 oz) caster (superfine) sugar
coconut oil, for frying

To make the lime and passion fruit curd, put the lime juice, passion fruit, sugar and butter in a heatproof bowl over a pan of simmering water. Stir until the butter has melted. Then, using a fork, stir in the beaten egg. Keep gently whisking the mixture (in one direction) over the heat for about 10 minutes until it has thickened like custard. Set aside.

To make the crêpes, mix together the rice flour, matcha, coconut milk, water and sugar in a bowl, making sure it is smooth and free of lumps. It should be the thickness of single cream.

Heat 1 teaspoon of coconut oil in a frying pan (skillet) over a medium–high heat. Add the peaches to brown for 2–3 minutes then, using a shallow ladle, spoon in a thin layer of the crêpe batter, swirling to cover the base of the pan. Cover with the lid for 1 minute, then remove the lid and cook for another minute, making sure the crêpe is crisp and golden. Place on a plate and spread a thin layer of the curd over the crêpe. Fold the crêpe in half, serve or set aside. Repeat this whole process until you have used all the ingredients.

Serve with the peaches and strawberries, or any other seasonal soft fruit, such as plums.

VIETNAMESE ICED COFFEE
CÀ PHÊ SỮA ĐÁ

Vietnamese coffee is among the best in the world. Along with baguettes, pastries and the alphabet, the now huge coffee culture was introduced by the French who colonised Vietnam for nearly 100 years. The coffee is usually from the darker, nutty robusta (sometimes chicory) beans, the chocolatey smell is so good in the mornings. My favourite way to have this is with ice, but you can also serve it hot, mix up the milk or leave the sweet milk to be had last. You will need a Vietnamese coffee filter per person.

Serves 1

2 tbsp (or more if desired) condensed milk
2 tbsp (or more if desired) medium or dark roast
    coarse ground coffee
handful of ice cubes

Pour the condensed milk into a glass, place the base of the coffee filter on top with the brewing chamber, then fill with coffee, gently tap and flatten to settle the grains with the filter insert as tight as possible, leave the insert on top. (Some filters may have a screw to tighten.) Fill a quarter with boiling water and wait 30 seconds for it to absorb and bloom then further fill with hot water to the top. Close the lid and wait for the coffee to slowly drip above the condensed milk in the glass for about 5 minutes. When it stops dripping, it is done. You can add more hot water to the filter or leave it strong.

Take the lid off and stand the coffee chamber onto it. Stir to combine the coffee and milk together then add ice cubes or pour the mixed coffee into a glass full of ice.

8   BASICS

n this section you'll find a treasure trove of useful recipes. From cooking perfect rice and noodles to pickles and dipping sauces, you will learn all of the easy basics.

STEAMED RICE

CƠM

Cooking rice is easy with a little experience. There isn't an exact rule as to the proportions of rice and water because there are lots of rice varieties and each will need a different amount of water. For Vietnamese jasmine rice grains, I use approximately 300 g (10½ oz) of rice and 500 ml (17 fl oz/2 cups) of water (serves 3–4). The aim is to get fluffy, cooked-just-right rice that isn't sticking together in clumps, or too soft or still hard. It is perfect when you can sink your teeth into it and it has a lovely mild nutty and floral rice flavour.

What we Asian kids learn from a very early age is to wash the rice first, about three times (three times is plenty – it is important not to over-wash the rice or it will lose flavour), in its cooking pot, running our fingers through the grains and slightly massaging them to release the starch. Then the starchy water is mostly poured out using the palm of your hands to catch the grains. The pot is then filled up with fresh water again to a level known with a couple of trials. To guide you, place your index finger just above the grains to measure halfway up the first crease for jasmine rice.

To cook rice, there is no better than in a simple rice cooker with two functions: cook and keep warm. It is a must-have and my most-used appliance.

When the rice is cooked, an important job for older kids is to fluff it up with a wooden or plastic paddle, by mixing and turning all the rice in the cooker around, then leaving it to rest in the cooker for a further 5–10 minutes.

If you don't have a rice cooker (you should get one), you will have to hover around the stove to watch over the pot. Cook the rice in a saucepan with a lid on a medium–low heat. When the water has seeped into the rice and there isn't any water on the surface, turn the heat to low and cook with the lid securely on to let the steam do its work for a further 15–18 minutes. Then turn off the heat without removing the lid and let it rest for 5–10 minutes. Fluff up the rice with a rice paddle or wooden spoon. (Unfortunately, you will often get a burnt bottom this way.)

Never ever boil your rice. What I mean is never cook it like pasta and then drain it as it will be wet, flat, not fluffy at all and then it will dry out.

Once you've mastered the fundamentals of plain steamed rice, there are many things you can do to rice on special occasions. Sometimes, I like to add some seasoning, like chicken stock instead of water, a garlic clove, a teaspoon of turmeric (see Hainan Chicken & Rice on page 34) or a good squeeze of ketchup (see Shaking Beef on page 77). It is also great to wash the grains, drain them and dry fry them with shallots and garlic before adding them to the rice cooker.

A meal isn't a real meal unless it comes with rice. Respect your rice. It is a staple, it makes the meal complete, and it will mean you will enjoy your food a lot more.

EGG FRIED RICE

CƠM CHIÊN TRỨNG

Egg fried rice is a simple nostalgic dish that is enjoyed by everyone whose ever loved a Chinese takeaway. The Vietnamese version by my mum is always laden with garlic, butter and black pepper. Its comfort and simplicity is unbeatable.

Knowing how to make egg fried rice is a simple and essential life skill, something that should just be cooked by heart.

I don't want to write a formal recipe for egg fried rice; it is something you do in the kitchen based on how much spare rice you have and adding a bit of this and a bit of that to your taste. Prepare everything first and work the hot wok quickly.

It is best to use cold leftover rice, refrigerated from the previous day. Simply fry off some chopped shallots and tantalising garlic in butter in a wok. Throw in frozen peas, canned sweetcorn or fresh cubed vegetables. Sometimes, it's lovely to use up that last slice of bacon, torn ham hock, leftover roast chicken or, better still, make an occasion of it with cubed spam (an inherited favourite from the Americans) – it is so good! So naughty! Very Vietnamese.

Flip over a container of cold rice into the wok. Using a wooden spoon or spatula, separate and flatten the rice, pour over soy sauce – the amount you think is right – and black pepper.

Fry until the rice is hot and evenly covered in sauce and ingredients. Taste and adjust your flavours. Finally, move the rice over to the edges of the wok, making a hollow in the centre, and break in an egg or two. Mix it up, throw in the desired amount of spring onions and/ or coriander, fold the egg in with the rice and continue to fry until it is all combined and you are satisfied. The rice shouldn't be wet or soggy.

STICKY RICE

XÔI ĐẬU XANH

Sticky rice can be flavoured and married with many other nutritious ingredients like mung beans, lentil, green beans, black-eyed peas, red kidney beans, Chinese sausage (okay not so nutritious but very delicious) and so on. It can be eaten as a savoury or sweet dish. It is fantastic cooked with pandan extract and coconut flakes, and served with fresh mango and coconut cream. Dunked in warm, sweet and treacly ginger syrup, it brings endless comfort.

It is best to soak the glutinous rice for at least an hour or overnight then steam; otherwise, it burns easily at the bottom and becomes soggy on top. But you can stick it in the rice cooker on occasions. Mix half glutinous and half jasmine rice with pre-soaked mung beans in a rice cooker and happily enjoy it with Braised Pork Belly & Eggs (page 26), Sticky Mustard & Marmalade Ribs (page 25) or Fried Chicken Wings (page 108).

Ideally, you will need a steamer for these sticky rice recipes.

Serves 2

5 tbsp glutinous rice
1 heaped tbsp split red lentils or split mung beans
pinch of sea salt
pinch of caster (superfine) sugar

Soak the rice and lentils in hot water for about an hour, then drain, season with salt and sugar and mix together well. Steam for 15–20 minutes until soft and sticky.

STICKY RICE WITH SHIITAKE & DRIED FIGS

XÔI CHAY

Serves 2

2 tbsp vegetable oil
200 g (7 oz/1 cup) glutinous rice, soaked in warm water for 1 hour, then drained
2 round shallots, sliced
20 g (¾ oz) fresh shiitake or a variety of wild mushrooms, sliced
pinch of sea salt
pinch of pepper
½ tsp caster (superfine) sugar
pinch of mushroom seasoning
60 g (2 oz) dried figs, sliced
1 spring onion (scallion), thinly sliced

Heat a frying pan (skillet) over a medium heat. Add the oil and brown off the shallots, then add the mushrooms and fry for 5 minutes. Add the mixture to the glutinous rice in a bowl with salt, pepper, sugar and mushroom seasoning and combine. Bring the water in a steamer to a boil. Place the rice mixture around the steamer, creating a hole for steam to flow in the middle. Steam for 30–40 minutes on a medium heat, making sure that you mix the rice around every 10 minutes so that steam is flowing evenly and checking that there is enough water in the base. At the end of the steaming time, leave in the steamer for another 10 minutes. When ready to serve, mix in the dried figs and spring onion.

You can also pack the sticky rice into banana leaf parcels which can be re-steamed or eaten at room temperature. Great for journeys, picnics and packed lunches.

RICE PORRIDGE

CHÁO

Cháo is a soup usually made from leftover cooked rice and is a light meal that is enjoyed any time throughout the day. It's also great when you're feeling under the weather because it's light, delicate and its added ingredients bring great healing power. A great feeling of comfort comes from eating this as a child – Vietnamese babies are weaned on it.

Making *cháo* is a great way to use leftover rice from the night before, and creating something healthy with herbs and vegetables we have to hand, like cubed vegetables such as carrots, courgettes, marrow and peas. For a stronger punch, use mustard leaves and watercress or milder spinach or kale for a subtle take. Be as creative as you wish by using simmered down rice using homemade chicken or pork stock, or a good-quality stock cube. Adapt this recipe according to the ingredients you have available.

The most popular ingredient in *cháo* is ginger, finely chopped down or minced with lean pork or chicken and spring onions. I like to add leaves and herbs, topped with leftover meat, ham, fish cake, or cook through a fillet of fish, such as salmon flakes for 5 minutes.

I have suggested a weight of leaves here but honestly, you can never have enough greens, so add as much as you like or as much as will fit in the pan. The cooked rice amount is also just a suggestion. The more rice you add, the thicker it may be so you might need to add more stock; the less you have the thinner it will be. Either way, it's all good.

Serves 2–3

220 g (7½ oz/1¼ cups) steamed rice (page 195)
750 ml (25 fl oz/3 cups) boiling water or homemade chicken stock
30 g (1 oz) ginger root, finely chopped
1 chicken or vegetable stock cube
1 tbsp fish sauce
pinch of freshly ground black pepper
50 g (2 oz) horseradish or mustard leaves, roughly sliced

For the garnish
1 spring onion (scallion), sliced
a few sprigs of coriander (cilantro), chopped
chillies or chilli oil (optional)
a squeeze of lime (optional)

Bring the steamed rice and water or stock to the boil in a saucepan, then cover and reduce to a simmer. Add the chopped ginger and stock cube and simmer for about 15–20 minutes, stirring occasionally so that it doesn't catch at the bottom. Over this cooking period, the rice will soften and expand into a porridge.

Season with the fish sauce and black pepper, then fold in the greens and cook until wilted. Serve in bowls with a choice of garnishes on top.

HOW TO
REHYDRATE NOODLES

To really enjoy Vietnamese, it is very important to cook your noodles to the right bite. Good texture is everything. Perfectly cooked noodles are neither under-cooked (too chewy) or over-cooked (soft, broken and soggy). Different dishes require different sized and shaped noodles. The type of noodle needed for each dish has stood the test of time but please use and adapt to what you can get hold of.

The instructions are easy but act as a guide. All brands and types of noodles will vary in their cooking time ever so slightly, so please take note of the packet instructions. Always use a timer. To get the noodles dry and fluffy, it is good to let them drain off in a colander and cover with a lid for 10–15 minutes.

Bánh canh/Japanese udon
Blanch in boiling water, gently separate the strands, for 1 minute, then drain.

Bánh hỏi/Sheets of fine rice vermicelli
These are really quick to prepare. Place about 8–10 sheets at a time in a bowl and submerge with boiling water from the kettle. Set the timer for 1 minute, then drain immediately. Leave to drain, steam off and dry for a few minutes, then place them onto a serving plate. You may need to do this in batches. Serve hot or at room temperature.

Bánh phở/Bún
Rice vermicelli (0.8 mm) or dry pho flat rice noodles
Rehydrate by placing them in a bowl, pour boiling water over them, cover and leave them to soak for 3-5 minutes. Drain, briefly wash with hot tap water in a sieve or colander, cover and leave to drain off.

Bánh phở tươi/Fresh pho flat rice noodles
Separate the strands and blanch in boiling water from the kettle for 1 minute if using with broth. If frying, simply separate the strands, then add to the frying pan (skillet).

Bún/Rice vermicelli (1.6 mm)
Bring a pot of water to the boil, cook the noodles for 10 minutes, turn off the heat, leave in the pot for 5–10 minutes, rinse in a colander until the starch water runs clear, cover and drain.

Mì/Fresh egg noodles
Either homemade or store-bought, these will fry much better and have more of a bite to them if you first air-dry them on a plate, turning them around after a couple of hours, then store them in an airtight container in the cupboard. When ready to use, blanch them in boiling water for a minute, rinse and drain before frying or assembling.

Miến/Glass noodles
The very fine glass noodles made from snow pea starch can be added to a small pot of broth for quick meals for one. Thicker glass noodles, made from arrowroot or sweet potato, need soaking in hot water for about 5–10 minutes, depending on size, until almost cooked but still with a bit of bite for further cooking. Once you have washed and drained them, they will fry easily. If they are for noodle soups, make sure they are cooked through with hot water.

FRESH HOMEMADE EGG NOODLES

MÌ TƯƠI

You will need a free-standing mixer for this recipe with a pasta attachment. If you don't have one, knead by hand and use a conventional pasta machine. If you mean business, you can roll it out with a rolling pin. Yikes!

Serves 3–4

200 g (7 oz) 00 pasta flour
2 large, free-range eggs
generous pinch of sea salt

Using an electric stand mixer with the dough hook attachment, add all the pasta ingredients to the bowl and knead to form a dough. Then leave in there, wrapped in beeswax wrap, to rest for 30 minutes at room temperature.

Once rested, knead again with the dough hook for 10 minutes, or until smooth. Tip the dough out onto the surface, roll into an even sausage and cut into four equal parts. Put the dough you are not using in an airtight container while rolling out each piece so it doesn't dry out.

Attach the rolling attachment to your stand mixer, or use a pasta machine and set it to the widest setting, usually number 1. Take one of the dough portions, pinch it into a rough rectangle and run through the widest setting six times, folding it in half after each roll, to smooth out the dough. Now begin to feed the dough through the settings each once through to number 6, or until thin to your liking. Dust flour on either side of the rolled-out dough and fold it over itself thee to four times ready to be sliced into noodle strands. Set aside and repeat with the remaining noodle dough.

Cut the noodle sheets into wide noodle strands by using a sharp knife and slicing roughly every 1 cm (½ in). Alternatively, run the sheets through the tagliatelle or spaghetti setting on your pasta machine. Lay the noodles out to dry or hang the noodles out to dry, turning occasionally and set aside in an airtight container until needed.

HOMEMADE CHIPS

KHOAI TÂY NƯỚNG

Serves 4

1.5 kg (3 lb 5 oz) potatoes, such as Maris Piper, peeled and sliced into chip shapes
2 garlic bulbs, unpeeled, sliced in half and bashed
2 tbsp vegetable oil or goose fat
sea salt and freshly ground black pepper

Preheat the oven to 180°C (350°F/gas 6). Put the potatoes in a large saucepan, cover with cold water and add a good pinch of salt. Bring to the boil for about 17 minutes, or until the potatoes are soft. Drain and leave in the colander to steam off.

Heat 2 tablespoons of oil or goose fat in a tray big enough to hold all the chips in the oven for about 10 minutes. Remove the hot tray from the oven, then spread the potatoes sticks evenly onto the tray; they should sizzle and hiss as they land. Spread the garlic around the tray and sprinkle with sea salt and black pepper. Bake for 45 minutes until golden, turning halfway through.

HOMEMADE BREADCRUMBS

VỤN BÁNH MÌ

Make as much as you'd like

stale bread

Preheat the oven to 140°C (280°F/gas 3).

Put the stale bread into a food processor and grind until fine. Spread evenly on a baking tray and bake for 12 minutes or until golden. Cool, then store in an airtight container to be used any time.

QUICK PICKLES
& OTHER TICKLES

DƯA CHUA

Pickles are an essential part of meals as they provide much of the sour element. You can make a quick pickle to go with many of the recipes in this book. Typically, carrot, daikon and kohlrabi are used to make pickles, but you can also use other crunchy vegetables, like radish, green papaya, celery, fennel, beetroot, cauliflower and so on.

Instant Carrot & Kohlrabi Pickle
Cà rốt và su hào ngâm chua

Makes 200 g (7 oz)

100 g (3½ oz) carrot, grated or julienne
100 g (3½ oz) kohlrabi or daikon, thinly sliced
    or julienned
1½ tbsp caster (superfine) sugar
2 tbsp cider vinegar

Thinly slice the vegetables into rounds and mix in a bowl with a good sprinkling of salt. Set aside for 15 minutes. In another bowl, mix the sugar and cider vinegar and pour over the vegetables. Leave for at least 30 minutes before serving.

Onion Pickle

Makes approx. 150 g (5 oz)

1 red or white onion, thinly sliced on a mandolin
2 tbsp cider vinegar or other good-quality vinegar
1 tbsp caster (superfine) sugar
1 tsp freshly ground black pepper

To make the onion pickle, place the onions into a medium bowl with the vinegar, sugar and black pepper.

Spring Onion Oil
Mỡ hành

Makes approx. 150 ml (5 fl oz)

2 tbsp oil
2 spring onions (scallions),
    white and green parts, sliced
pinch of sea salt

Put the oil and spring onions in a small saucepan over a low heat and cook with a small pinch of salt, stirring occasionally, for 5 minutes, then remove from the heat.

Crispy Shallots
Hành phi

Makes approx. 150 g (5 oz)

6 round shallots, thinly sliced
2 tbsp vegetable oil

Fry the shallots in the oil over a low heat until golden, then remove from the heat and drain (saving the oil). Leave to dry on kitchen paper. The shallots will continue to brown and crisp. Save the flavourful oil and crispy shallots in two separate containers for future uses with noodle soups and to top up rice, noodles and salads.

FISH SAUCES

NƯỚC MẮM

Nước chấm is the northern term for dipping sauce. In the south, we call it *nước mắm* and the sauce varies to suit every meal. Be it a simple fish sauce with crushed chillies or an extravaganza of sweet, sour, salty, umami, hot and bitter flavours from a variety of those tasting ingredients.

When making a *nước mắm*, remember to trust your taste buds entirely and try to get the right balance at all times. If you think about it, many Vietnamese dishes are simply cooked, it is only when it is complemented with a beautiful sauce that everything marries together, so it's really important you get your sauces right.

Use a knife to finely chop or a mortar and pestle to crush chillies, garlic, ginger or lemongrass together, combine the mixture with something sweet and something sour. Shake it up in a jar, use a hand blender or simply mix it together in a bowl with a spoon.

Feel free to leave out or adjust hotness of chillies and pungent garlic for young children, and replace sugar with honey, maple syrup, agave nectar, coconut syrup or anything sweet and syrupy. You can use lemon or lime juice instead of vinegar but also use any interesting vinegars you come across. You can add finely chopped lemongrass, crushed ginger, a variety of blended nuts, coriander (cilantro) stalks or chopped mint, sesame seeds, puréed mango and other juices. Simmer seasonal fruits like plums, raspberries or gooseberries with sugar, like making a compote then add that to a *nước mắm*.

Most importantly, always use a premium fish sauce for your sauces. Always! Use these as templates to change up elements and flavour notes with different ingredients when it suits.

Fish Sauce
Nước mắm

Serves 4

2 bird's eye chillies, finely chopped
2 garlic cloves, crushed
3 tbsp caster (superfine) sugar
3 tbsp white wine vinegar
4 tbsp fish sauce
80 ml (2½ fl oz/5 tbsp) hot water

Mix all the ingredients together well.

Sweet Chilli & Garlic Dipping Sauce
Nước mắm chua ngọt

This is a thicker and more intense sauce to dip or pour over protein dishes like Fried Brill (page 44) or Crispy Roast Pork Belly (page 98). I like to add a herbal element and use lime or lemon juice to create invigorating and refreshing tastes.

Serves 4

1 bird's eye chilli, finely chopped
1 garlic clove, crushed
2 tbsp maple syrup (or honey, agave nectar, coconut syrup, marmalade or caster (superfine) sugar)
2 tbsp fish sauce
finely chopped zest and juice of ½ lime or lemon
sprig of mint leaves, thinly sliced
a few coriander (cilantro) stalks, thinly sliced

Prepare the dipping sauce by adding all the ingredients and shaking together in a jar.

Sweet Chilli & Mango Sauce
Nước mắm xoài

This goes well with lots of dishes, especially English Night Fish & Chips (page 111).

Serves 4

2 bird's eye chillies with seeds, finely chopped
zest of 1 lime, finely chopped
1½ tbsp lime juice
½ ripe mango, puréed with hand blender
2 tbsp maple syrup
2 tbsp fish sauce

Blend all the ingredients together in a small blender or with a hand blender.

Ginger Dipping Sauce
Nước mắm gừng

Serves 4

20 g (¾ oz) ginger root, finely chopped or grated
2 garlic cloves, finely chopped or blended
2 bird's eye chillies, with or without seeds
3 tbsp lime juice
3 tbsp maple syrup
4 tsp fish sauce

To make the ginger dipping sauce, grind together the ginger, garlic and chillies in a mortar and pestle to a smooth paste, then mix together with the lime juice, maple syrup and fish sauce.

SOY SAUCES

NƯỚC SỐT TƯƠNG

As with all the *nước chấm* dressings, you need to follow the sweet, sour, salty, umami, hot and bitter rules to satisfy your taste buds when making soy-based sauces. Soy-based sauces pair really well with nutty umami ingredients like tahini and nut butters such as peanut, cashew and almond, miso, hoisin and fruit purées such as plum. You can make a soy-based sauce and pour over fried noodles and stir-fry with vegetables to make a truly pleasurable plant-based meal or snack. Blend, shake or stir all the ingredients together.

Tahini & Soy Sauce
Nước sốt tương bơ mè

Tahini pairs really well with soy sauces. However, if you don't have tahini, it can be replaced with lots of different types of nut butters and plant-based condiments to make a great sauce for dipping and cooking with. Try simmering sweet peeled plums, apricot and nectarines to use instead of sugar. You can also make it more savoury by adding a teaspoon of miso and Japanese ponzu (a citrus-based sauce) or yuzu (a citrus fruit), for the sour element. Feel free to add chopped herbs.

Serves 4

1 bird's eye chilli, finely chopped
1 garlic clove, crushed
1 tbsp caster (superfine) sugar
1 tbsp lime or lemon juice, plus zest of 1 lime,
    finely chopped
2½ tbsp soy sauce
2½ tbsp tahini

Shake all the ingredients together in a jar.

Notes   ♦ Add a teaspoon of miso, a little
          soy sauce and chilli to ring the
          changes.

Honey & Lemon Soy Sauce
Nước tương chanh mật ong

I find this is the most popular soy sauce among guests – it enhances all kinds of salads.

Serves 4

1 bird's eye chilli, finely chopped
1 tbsp clear runny honey
1 tbsp lemon juice
2½ tbsp soy sauce

Just shake all the ingredients together in a jar.

INFUSIONS

TRÀ

Make a pot of tea to keep you hydrated throughout the day and maximise your ingredients with leftover mint, ginger, lemongrass, pandan and vegetables. Don't waste a thing. These are nice as hot or cold drinks. I keep infusions in my flask to drink throughout the day or have a hot pot standing by at my desk.

Ginger
Revitalise and stimulate your senses with a good cup of refreshing ginger tea with freshly peeled and sliced ginger. A whole thumb is adequate for two in a teapot. This infusion helps aid digestion and can be enjoyed with meals. It will perk you up when you're feeling under the weather too.

Lemongrass
Re-root the ends of lemongrass in a glass of water and drink the shoots that regrow quickly. You can also bash half a stalk with the back of a knife and infuse in boiling water. Pairs well with fresh ginger.

Lime or lemon
Hot lemon with or without honey is universal goodness. Infuse with slices of zest.

Pandan
Seep a couple of knots or sliced pandan leaves in hot water to make a soothing and comforting drink.

Vegetables
Save the water from poaching organic vegetables and drink it hot or cold.

MENU IDEAS

ĂN CƠM – THINGS WE EAT WITH RICE, FAMILY STYLE

For these menus, take a recipe from any chapter and add at least one sharing vegetable dish.

It's traditional to have a soup like the Watercress, Ginger & Pork Rib Soup (page 135) or Sea Bass in Tomato, Celery & Dill Broth (page 40). Fill your bowl with broth from the centre of the table in between rice servings, drinking up all the grains. Share everything and keep taking from the sharing plates instead of taking it all in one go at the start. Eat the dishes in any order you like.

A lot of the recipes like Chicken Curry with Squash (page 30), Braised Pork Belly & Eggs in Coconut Water (page 26), Caramelised Hake with Fish Sauce & Ginger (page 38) and Slow-cooked Beef with Lemongrass, Star Anise & Root Vegetables (page 23) can be made ahead and keep well for delicious midweek dinners when you're pressed for time. They are also great for dinner parties, too.

Ăn Cơm – Things We Eat With Rice, Family Style 1
Fried Brill on Watercress with a Chilli-Lime Sweet & Sour Sauce (page 44)
Sea Bass in Tomato, Celery & Dill Broth (page 40)
Chayotes & Garlic (page 68)
Steamed Rice (page 195)

Ăn Cơm – Things We Eat With Rice, Family Style 2
Caramelised Hake with Fish Sauce & Ginger (page 38)
Hot & Fiery Greens with Anchovies (page 65)
Watercress, Ginger & Pork Rib Soup (page 135)
Steamed Rice (page 195)

Ăn Cơm – Things We Eat With Rice, Family Style 3
Braised Pork Belly & Eggs in Coconut Water (page 26)
Chicken Broth from Hainan Chicken & Rice (page 34)
Runner Beans & Celery Leaves with Garlic (page 54)
Steamed Rice (page 195)

Ăn Cơm – Things We Eat With Rice, Family Style 4
Ginger Chicken (page 32)
Sea Bass in Tomato, Celery & Dill Broth (page 40)
Sautéed Mushrooms & Jerusalem Artichoke (page 56)
Sticky Rice (page 199)

Ăn Cơm – Things We Eat With Rice, Family Style 5
Sea Bass Parcels with Ginger & Kimchi (page 43)
Soy Aubergines & Thai Basil (page 58)
Fried Watercress, Pea Shoots & Tahini (page 62)
Steamed Rice (page 195)

CELEBRATIONS & PARTIES

You can create a buffet of food ready for hungry pickers to fill their plates with these favourites. These sit well at room temperature.

Fried Chicken Wings (page 108)

Crispy Roast Pork Belly (page 98)

Fresh Salad Rolls (page 88)

Seafood Spring Rolls (page 112)

Papaya Salad with Pork Belly, Prawns & Pomelo (page 86)

Shaking Beef with Watercress Salad & Tomato Rice (page 77)

Fried Noodles & Greens (page 159)

Orange & Lime Baked Cheesecake (page 183)

With small dinner parties, you can show guests how to roll fresh rolls with an array of ingredients and nominate a helper to roll up sizzling crêpes. It's a great icebreaker and fun way to spend time with friends and family, while also showing them exciting new flavours. For dinner parties, I always think about how long things take to do and if there are particular recipes I can prep ahead of time so that I am not flustered when guests have arrived.

Dinner Parties 1
Fresh Salad Rolls (page 88)
Sizzling Crêpes with Prawns (page 84)
Duck & Bamboo Noodle Soup (page 140)
Pandan Ice Cream (page 174)

Dinner Parties 2
Seafood Spring Rolls (page 112)
Lemongrass Beef Noodle Soup (page 130)
Fried Courgette Flowers with Prawns & Chives (page 70)
Coconut Rice Pudding with Ginger Syrup & Grilled Peaches (page 178)

Dinner Parties 3
Fresh Salad Rolls (page 88)
Chicken Salad with Sugar Snap Peas, Vietnamese Coriander & Shallots (page 78)
Crispy Roast Pork Belly (page 98)
Coconut & Mango Pudding with Sago Tapioca Balls (page 180)

Dinner Parties 4
Fried Chicken Wings (page 108)
Singapore Fried Noodles with Purple Sprouting Broccoli (page 160)
Hainan Chicken & Rice (page 34)
Cassava Cake (page 176)

ACKNOWLEDGEMENTS

To Olive, my beautiful daughter and biggest love; you are everything to me. I hope these recipes will grow with you and live with you.

I am truly grateful to my family, friends, neighbours and all those on social media across the world from London, to Rome, to Kuala Lumpa, Sydney and California who have tested these recipes and sent back their in-depth feedback and details to help make the recipes in this book work with better ease and tastiness. Without the love and care that went on, I doubt I would have managed. This gave me a better understanding of what is accessible, how to word instructions and see how the recipes are read, understood and executed. Thank you with all my heart for your patience, efforts, dedication and willingness.

Thank you to Kate Pollard who commissioned me to write this book. I wholeheartedly trust your sense of style and design and hope I did this some justice. Thank you Rosie Birkett, my old friend, and life traveller who introduced me to Hardie Grant. Thank you to my friends, Kylee Newton and Melissa Hemsley for always helping, for always pushing and encouraging me to step forward.

Thank you to Eila Purvis and all at Hardie Grant for your patience and understanding of this work. We did this without ever meeting each other – not even a Zoom call – but I feel your presence by my side throughout our editing journey. Thank you to Ruth Tewkesbury for taking me on another journey after I have typed these words to land this book onto many kitchen surfaces. Thank you to Stephanie Moon in San Francisco for your help with the US publicity and for taking time to listen to my stories and ideas. Love how we can dream big. Thank you to Wendy Hobson for thrifting through the number of teaspoons and millilitres of fish sauce in this book. Thank you to my sister-in-law, My Luu, for the Vietnamese translations and for your continual love, strength, support and patience.

Thank you to Evi O., Susan Le and Nicole Ho in Sydney for the amazing designs and illustrations. It's such a dream to have worked with you – I love how you've captured the spirit of the book.

It was wonderful to shoot with Aya Nishimura who styled this book with such conviction and stance. Thank you for your care and dedication. Thank you Laurie Noble, for taking the pictures when I am in them and always your help and convo.

Thank you to Chris Howgate for colour grading my photography.

Thank you to my closest friends, Agnieszka Makulska, Fatima Mouzo, Anja Siemens, Sophie Dening, Nobuko Yoneyama, Will Timbers and Claudia Martello for your bottomless love, support and encouragement from every picket line.

Thank you to Ben Ridolfi and Phil Derham at Park District for always believing in me, taking chances, making nice films, animation and stills together. For always letting me borrow what I need, teaching me things I don't know and being such a fabulous team to work with.

Thank you to James O Jenkins, for your love and support throughout and every day along the way. You are such a wonderful father to our daughter who has inherited your wit, charm and kindness. Thank you for taking care of her so that I can write this book and for giving Kodi the dog his voice. I love it when you use these recipes to cook for us. I love you and Olive so much.

Most of all, thank you to my mum, Má Nga, the pillar of strength and kindness who has taught me what good food is all about. Thank you for sacrificing everything for me and Cu Toon, my brother, and for always being there for us no matter what. Who knew that when we were refugees we would have our own takeaway business 40 years later. Be thankful and make the most and the best of everything you're given you'd say.

Thank you to all of the many people who have visited my supper club, cooking classes and ordering my takeaways; I am so grateful for your continued support and all the smiles you bring. Thank you! Hopefully more soon.

ABOUT THE AUTHOR

Uyen Luu was 5 years old when she came to England in the early 80s with her mother and brother as refugees from post-war Vietnam. She was raised and went to school in North London then went on to study Film & Video at Central Saint Martins. After graduating, she was awarded a grant from The Arts Council of England to return to Vietnam for the first time and make a 16mm documentary film about going home, Phở (Noodle Soup). The film toured the UK, European and world festival circuit and won Best Documentary at the Karlovy Vary International Film Festival in 2001.

Uyen went on to open a fashion and lifestyle boutique in Seven Dials, Covent Garden. For almost 10 years, she went back and forth to Saigon, eating the most delicious food along the way while she was designing and hand producing her clothing brand Leluu with her cousin Thúy and her friends.

It was only when she moved out of her family home and she began to miss her mother's cooking that she started to cook Vietnamese for her friends, and write a blog about it. In 2009, Uyen started a supper club, cooking food she learnt and ate on her travels.

Uyen wrote her first book *My Vietnamese Kitchen* in 2013 and is a regular contributor in *The Observer Food Monthly* and *The Guardian*. Her love of food, film and photography led to a career in food styling and food photography.

Since having her daughter, Uyen has hosted the supper clubs and Vietnamese cooking classes at her photography studio in Hackney. After 10 years, this had to come to a pause because of the pandemic and has been re-adapted to takeaways (takeouts). It was during this time that she wrote *Vietnamese*, with the hope that it would help lots of people cook Vietnamese with ease and pleasure.

Uyen lives with her daughter Olive, her partner James and Kodi the dog in North London.

@loveleluu
www.uyenluu.com

INDEX

Published in 2021 by Hardie Grant Books,
an imprint of Hardie Grant Publishing

Hardie Grant Books (London)
5th & 6th Floors
52–54 Southwark Street
London SE1 1UN

Hardie Grant Books (Melbourne)
Building 1, 658 Church Street
Richmond, Victoria 3121

hardiegrantbooks.com

British Library Cataloguing-in-Publication Data.
A catalogue record for this book is available from
the British Library.

Vietnamese
ISBN: 978-1-78488-423-9

10 9 8 7 6 5 4

Publisher: Kajal Mistry
Editor: Eila Purvis
Design and Art Direction: Evi O. Studio |
Evi O., Nicole Ho & Susan Le
Illustrations: Evi O. Studio | Susan Le
Photographer: Uyen Luu
Camera Assistant and Additional Photography
on pages 103, 139, 156, 163, 203, 213 and 219:
Laurie Noble
Food Stylist: Aya Nishimura and Uyen Luu
Food Stylist on page 83: Rosie Ramsden
Food Stylist on page 120: Joanna Resiak
Home Economist: Nga Le
Prop Stylist: Aya Nishimura and Tabitha Hawkins
Copy-editor: Wendy Hobson
Proofreader: Sarah Herman
Indexer: Cathy Heath
Production Controller: Nikolaus Ginelli

Colour reproduction by p2d
Printed and bound in China
by Leo Paper Products Ltd.

MIX
Paper from
responsible sources
FSC™ C020056